JOE,

HOPE YOU ENJOY
"ALFRED'S LUCKY CHARM"
ON PAGE 78.

GOOD HUNTING,
JEFF

Hunting
Camp Journal

NORTH AMERICAN HUNTING CLUB
MINNETONKA, MINNESOTA

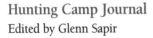

Hunting Camp Journal
Edited by Glenn Sapir

Mike Vail
Vice President, Product & Business Development

Tom Carpenter
Director of Book Development

Dan Kennedy
Book Production Manager

Heather Koshiol
Jen Guinea
Book Development Coordinators

Beowulf
Book Design and Production

Photo Credits
All photos by authors except: Phil Aarestad, cover onlay; Tom Carpenter, NAHC, 16, 177; Bill Marchel, 1; NAHC, 164; Ol' Man Treestands, 19; Ralston Purina, 102, 105; Glenn Sapir, 3; Bryce Towsley, 185.

Illustrations: Larry Anderson, 9, 27, 42, 52, 60, 73, 83, 88, 92, 95, 101, 119, 121, 127, 130, 143, 149, 154, 162, 170, 171, 192; Jeff Boehler, 79; National Bowhunters Education Foundation, 145.

ISBN 1-58159-102-0

1 2 3 4 5 6 7 8 / 03 02 01 00

ESCAPE ... WITH THE HUNTING CAMP JOURNAL

Everybody needs to escape now and again.

As hunters, we have the great fortune of being able to live one of the greatest escapes of all, every time we go hunting. To be afield, hunting again, does something for the soul that no other activity can compare to. It's probably safe to say that a universal truth among hunters is this: It is better to have hunted, no matter what the outcome, than not to have hunted at all!

But hunting seasons come and go. There are gaps between spring turkey season, summer varmint hunts, early fall bowhunts, small game season, forays to fields and wetlands for birds and waterfowl, the rifle season for deer, the trip Out West or Up North or Down South or To The Cabin … How do you escape for awhile when you're *not* hunting?

That's where this *Hunting Camp Journal* comes in. No matter how busy you are, there's always time to pick it up, read a few pages and be transported out to the woods, hills, mountains, fields or wetlands.

Glenn Sapir

Whether you take it to hunting camp or enjoy it at home before, during or after the season, this journal is packed with hunting entertainment, insights and ideas.

Editor Glenn Sapir has brought it all together—tales and tips, woodsmanship, game profiles, hunting stories, recipes, humor and more—in one fun, easy-reading package. Pull up an easy chair, or a camp bunk, and enjoy some journal entries anytime. You don't have to read the whole book at once!

Need to get away for just a little while? Keep your *Hunting Camp Journal* handy, and let it take you wherever you need to go.

3

CONTENTS

Here's a guide to the wide variety of hunting and outdoor topics you'll find in this *Hunting Camp Journal.*

ALL IN FUN

ALL IN FUN: Huntin' camp should be fun. It's a time to play cards, tell tales and share laughs. Hunting camp is also a place where you and your buddies test skills and knowledge.

Here is some easy reading, full of interesting facts, challenging quizzes, funny stories and cartoons that will probably put a grin on your face—the right prescription for huntin' camp.

FAVORITE HUNTS

FAVORITE HUNTS: What makes a hunt one to be remembered? Of course, a large game animal that we harvest is one answer. A memorable hunt, however, can be because of the people with whom we hunted, the country that we traversed or the conditions under which the hunt transpired.

Here are some memorable hunts you'll want to go on. They are hunts that bring insight to different cultures, that bring father and son even closer together and show how endurance can pay off with prize game animals.

Enjoy these memorable hunts. They'll probably get you thinking about some of your very own favorite excursions afield.

GAME PROFILES

Game Profiles: You can never know enough about the game you're hunting. And if you truly love what you hunt—and most of us do—you'll never tire of reading and learning about that animal or bird.

So here are details you can put to work, facts you want and need to know: How much does a cow elk weigh? When do pronghorns rut? What do moose eat? How the heck do you hunt sheep, anyway?

The details here will take you right out into the field—wherever these great game animals roam—and expand your knowledge with facts you need and want to know. You'll come away with more knowledge, and that will make you a better and even more successful hunter.

GETTING READY

GETTING READY: An important part of the hunting experience takes place at home and at camp. That's where preparation of equipment takes place. It is also where preparation of your game may happen. Home and camp is also where a lot of learning occurs, whether it comes from conversations with your fellow hunters, from videotapes or from magazines and books.

Here are a lot of handy tips that will help make your time getting ready an important part of the hunting experience.

RECIPES

Recipes: We've all experienced it, and we'll all do it again: We've walked up to game we've shot and thought: "Well, I've done it. Now I've got to eat this baby." Game meat of all kinds is as flavorful and good-for-you as any other meat on earth—probably better, in fact, on both counts. But who has enough ideas to keep the variety flowing through your kitchen and across your grill?

Everybody needs help with game cooking ideas now and again, so we've come to the rescue. We've sprinkled plenty of recipes throughout these pages, offering dozens of ideas that you can steal and make your own. Go ahead!

Whether it's in camp or back at home, make the most of all the game you shoot. It is the best meat around, and these recipe ideas will help you keep it all interesting.

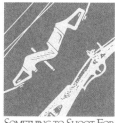

SOMETHING TO SHOOT FOR

SOMETHING TO SHOOT FOR: Why do we love to look at the photos of other people's successes? A lot of responses could answer that question.

For example, when they are shots of fellow North American Hunting Club members, we feel a happiness for those in our "fraternity."

There is also the "if they can do it, maybe someday I will too" attitude. These wonderful harvests truly do give us something to shoot for.

Most of all, we like to dream, putting ourselves in the picture with the game we may someday harvest. We learn from others' successes: Where did they get their game? What did they use? Did they hunt with a guide or outfitter, and if they did, who was it? Seeing what our fellow hunters have done, where and how they've done it and with whom they hunted is all information that we can integrate into our hunting plans.

TIPS AFIELD

Tips Afield: If anybody knew it all, he or she would be the guru of all hunters. Truth is, however, that hunting knowledge comes from a variety of sources, because no single person has a lock on hunting knowledge.

Learn from a number of experts—hunting equipment manufacturers, hunting organizations, outdoor celebrities and fellow members of the North American Hunting Club—how you can make the most of your experience afield.

Don't Let "Someday" Slip Away

FAVORITE HUNTS

BY GLENN SAPIR

*t*hink long and hard before you turn down an invitation to go hunting with a friend. I do—now!

Norm Strung, of Bozeman, Montana, was a friend. Perhaps you knew him, or his work, for he wrote about the outdoors for many magazines. As a New York-based magazine editor, I knew Norm as a writer who would always deliver his work on deadline and in an informative and readable style. As a member of the Outdoor Writers Association of America (OWAA), I knew Norm as a hard worker, who never said no to volunteering his time and labor. Unfortunately, I didn't know Norm as a hunting or fishing companion.

"When are you going to come out and spend some time with me?" he would ask each year we were together at the OWAA conference.

"We'll do it someday," I'd say to him, just as I did to several other members who offered similarly gracious invitations.

One June Norm didn't come to the OWAA conference—laid up by a hernia operation, I was told. In truth, the hernia was a malignant tumor. By October, Norm was dead.

I grieved for Norm and his wife, Sil. His passing stirred regrets about other unfulfilled relationships. So, I phoned Bill McRae; our friendship had roots similar to Norm's and mine.

"Let's go deer hunting next fall," I emphatically suggested to Bill. I was determined to call in some of those long-standing invitations.

I left the where and when to Bill. The only thing important to me was that we be together, away from desks, telephones and meetings.

Bill had long ago established himself as a premier wildlife photographer and in more recent years had emerged as a successful writer. As an editor, I had tapped into both of those talents. As fellow board-of-director members of OWAA, we had shared many conferences. We had, however, never hunted together.

On November 7, a year after my call to him, Bill was greeting me at the Great Falls, Montana, airport.

"Good to see you," we said as we shook hands with our right and hugged with our left. We split up my luggage and toted it out to Bill's big 4-wheel-drive, then headed east on Highway 200 in a wet snowfall.

For five hours we talked. That year, the presidential campaign was recent history, so we spoke a lot about the state

6

of the country. I discovered that Bill belonged to the same political party as I, that he had voted for the same candidate, and that we shared a lot of the same views on how to cure the country's ills. I learned about the tragic death of his son in a riverboat accident in Alaska, and we talked about how his wife Mary's new Postal Service job was working out. We also tread on less weighty topics, and, as we always did when together, we unmercifully shot good-natured barbs at each other. Such conversation doesn't come up when an editor request is an article on binoculars or a slide of bighorn rams from a contributor—and that, more than a trophy mule deer, is why I went to Montana.

We pulled into Keith Atcheson's Sand Springs trailer camp just shy of midnight. The snow hadn't let up since we first set out, and I could feel some of the tension unwind from Bill's neck and shoulders as he pulled off the slick, wet highway and slid out of the vehicle.

Our eventual destination was the Missouri Breaks, an hour or two northeast of Sand Springs. We were scheduled to head for camp the next day, but when tomorrow came, Keith passed down word to Bill, me and the other three hunters.

"We can't get into the Breaks today," said Keith. "The mud just won't let us do it."

The area had experienced an unusual amount of precipitation, and the normally hard soil had become Missouri River gumbo, a thick, black mud.

So, leaving our guns in camp, we drove the highway looking for deer and pronghorns in the rolling prairie parted by the paved road. Bill told me about a game he used to play with his kids when taking long drives.

"Deer and antelope were worth 25 cents," he explained, "grizzly bears 5 dollars. Whoever spotted them first earned that amount."

Spotting a couple of herds of pronghorns offset the few muleys I'd seen and quickly put Bill up a couple of dollars.

Next day, despite the muddy conditions, Keith decided to move the caravan of 4WDs into the Breaks. Travel was

Continued ...

slow once we left the hardtop, and Bill's vehicle threatened to leave the road a couple times.

When we finally pulled into our M*A*S*H*-like tent camp, Bill and I moved our gear into the simply furnished tent, then took a sightseeing hike while the guides and outfitter got camp up to snuff.

Camp was a mile or two from the Missouri River, or, more properly, Fort Peck Reservoir, which the nearest stretch of the Missouri is called. Though the rolling hills began to take on harsher and more abrupt changes in elevation, they gave only an occasional hint of the severely broken topography that lay closer to the water and gave the Missouri Breaks their name.

When we got back to camp, Bill Drew informed Bill and me that he'd be guiding us for the couple of hours before nightfall. Shouldering our packs and rifles, Bill and I followed Drew, who showed no mercy for the slow of foot. We covered a lot of ground quickly, and I was tempted to whisper to the guide that Bill, who at 58 at the time was 14 years my senior and in top physical shape, had a heart condition or some other fictional ailment by which I could enjoy the adjustment without incurring any of the blame.

The longer we walked, however, the easier it was to keep pace. We spotted mule deer literally miles away, but too far for a stalk that evening. With dark-ness threatening, we worked our way back to camp.

Next morning, at first light, Nate Nehls ferried Drew and me across Fort Peck Reservoir in one of the jetboats he brought upriver before the season. Believe it or not, the details of the hunt are less significant to me than the quality time I spent with Bill McRae. I got my buck the first day.

Bill was there waiting for the boat to pull in that day; Nehls's radio had forewarned him that I'd downed a deer. Bill greeted me with a smile and a handshake, similar to when we first started our trip at the airport. Back at camp, we relived the experience. Later in the week, I accompanied Bill when he downed a buck off a 250-yard shot at dawn.

The hunting trip ended with my priorities fulfilled and in order: I went home at least in as good of shape as when I left; I enjoyed the company of a special friend; and I shot a magnificent mule deer buck. No, the deer wouldn't make the record book, maybe not even a lot of hunters' walls, but for me it would be a reminder of a worthy challenge, new acquaintances and a friend's invitation that was too important to pass up.

White-Tailed Deer

ODOCOILEUS VIRGINIANUS

OTHER NAMES:

Whitetail, Virginia deer

CHARACTERISTICS:

Coat grayish-brown in winter, reddish-brown in summer; underside of foot-long tail white; antlers consist of main beams, generally with three to five tines projecting upward; brow tines long; outside of lower hind foot has a small, teardrop-shaped scent gland. Mature bucks weigh 100 pounds depending on good range, does 75 to 150 pounds.

HABITAT:

Almost anywhere food and a little cover exist; from conifer to hardwood forests; farmland; swamps; river- and creekbottoms; suburban areas.

FOOD:

Crops, leaves, twigs, fruits and berries of browse plants such as oak, chokecherry, serviceberry, snowberry and willow; some grasses and forbs from spring through fall.

BEHAVIOR:

Occupy small home ranges, do not migrate far; mostly nocturnal and secretive; solitary much of the time but form small groups in favored feeding areas. When alarmed or running, they erect and wag their tails causing white underside to flash.

REPRODUCTION:

Breed mid- to late-November; one or two reddish but white-spotted fawns; bucks do not gather harems; necks of rutting bucks swell; healthy adult bucks shed antlers in December or January; does usually breed first as yearlings (16 to 17 months), but in many areas as fawns.

HUNTING:

Our most command popular big game animal, but also our most elusive. Most whitetails are shot by hunters on stands who pay careful attention to details—wind direction, stand selection, keeping movement and fidgeting to a minimum.

Recipes

Big Game Jerky

Ingredients

1 to 2 lbs. venison or big game steak
$^{1}/_{2}$ cup imported soy sauce
Garlic salt

Preparation

Slice steak with grain no more than $^{1}/_{4}$-inch wide and no more than $^{1}/_{2}$-inch thick. Dip strips in soy sauce and place on a rack in a 2-inch-deep oven pan. Sprinkle generously with garlic salt. Put into a 150 to 175°F oven for 10 to 12 hours. Halfway through the cooking time, turn jerky pieces over. Jerky will keep indefinitely, and no refrigeration is needed.

NRA Recipe

Venison Jerky

Ingredients

2 lbs. thinly sliced ($^{1}/_{4}$-inch thick) lean venison
1 tbsp. black pepper
1 tbsp. onion powder
1 tbsp. garlic salt

1 tsp. liquid smoke
$^{1}/_{4}$ cup soy sauce
$^{1}/_{4}$ cup Worcestershire sauce
Cayenne pepper to taste

Preparation

Combine all ingredients, mixing thoroughly. Let marinade in refrigerator for 8 to 24 hours. Remove and place strips on dehydrator until they bend and crack without breaking.

Robert L. Brewer Jr.
Knoxville, TN

Ten Camo Tips

Haas Outdoors, manufacturer of Mossy Oak brand camouflage, offers these ten important tips on camouflage:

1 Match pattern to background, and consider wearing a different pattern on top and bottom.

2 Always use camo on your hands and face. Many hunters dress in full camouflage and fail to cover their hands and face. These parts move more than any other during hunting.

3 Cover anything shiny. For example: your watch, buttons, snaps and zippers. These small details demand great attention.

4 Purchase pants that are two to three inches longer than normal. This will keep light-colored socks and boots from standing out.

5 Wear boots with dark soles. Footwear is sometimes the first thing an animal will see if the hunter is sitting at ground level.

6 Avoid direct sunlight. If possible, face west in the morning and east in the afternoon.

7 Think about your intentions when you pick a spot to sit down. Within 40 yards you want to blend. From 40 yards out you want to concentrate on breaking your outline.

8 Set up on edges; avoid getting in the middle of thick cover. This hampers your vision as well as your chances of seeing game that travels the edges.

9 Keep your outline as low as possible. Avoid an animal's eye level. Scrunch down while on the ground, and get 15 feet or higher when using a treestand.

10 Use face paint to touch up around your eyes, even if you wear a face net. It keeps the shine down.

WILD TURKEY

NAME:
Bob Branton

RESIDENCE:
Boyne City, MI

WHERE TAKEN:
Northwestern Michigan

ARMS USED:
PSE Bow; Easton Arrow with Satellite
Titan 100 Broadhead

*Bob's Eastern wild turkey brought the
scales down to 21 pounds, and the beard
stretched the measuring tape to 9^1/$_2$ inches.*

NAME:
Robert Evans

RESIDENCE:
Chanhassen, MN

WHERE TAKEN:
Illinois

*Robert took this beauty on Crooked
Creek Whitetail Properties.*

What's Wrong With My Shotgun Pattern ?

Over the years there has been a great variety of "correct depths" used for shotgun chambers, many of them shorter than the $2^3/4$- to $3^1/2$-inch overall fired length of today's plastic hulls.

Couple this with a short forcing cone—the taper from chamber diameter to bore diameter—and you've got a performance problem. The crimp must have sufficient room to unfold completely flat when the shot and wad go from hull to bore or the results are deformed shot, distorted patterns, excessive recoil and pressure.

According to Joe Ventimiglia of Venco Industries, any older gun that isn't shooting well with today's shells might need to have the chamber and force cone lengthened by a competent gunsmith.

"Just a little adjustment," he suggests, "can make a tremendous difference in patterning, recoil and performance."

What Is Gauge Anyway?

Ever wonder what the terms "12 gauge," "20 gauge" and other gauges refer to?

According to Frank Ventimiglia of Venco Industries, the system of grading shotgun bore sizes was developed long ago, when a gun's size was determined by the weight of the largest lead ball that would fit the bore.

"If it took 12 of those balls to weigh 1 pound, you had a 12 gauge gun. If the ball that fit the bore was smaller, and it took 20 to weigh a pound, your gun was a 20 gauge."

The exception to this is the .410, which is named after its normal bore diameter of .410 inches. If it had been named like the larger shotguns, it would be a 67.5 gauge gun.

HUNTING HUMOR

ALL IN FUN

Tomasic art

"Go out there and help
your father bring in the groceries."

Then & Now

*W*hen it comes to populations of many game animals, the good old days are now. See how close you can come to estimating the nationwide numbers of the following species, both years ago and today, based on figures provided by the National Shooting Sports Foundation.

WHITE-TAILED DEER

1. In 1900, fewer than _____ white-tails remained in the nation.
   A. $^1/_2$ million B. 1 million
   C. 2 million D. 5 million
2. Today, conservation programs have returned the whitetail population to more than _____.
   A. 6 million B. 10 million
   C. 14 million D. 18 million

CANADA GEESE

3. Habitat destruction reduced Canada goose populations to a low of some _____ in the 1940s.
   A. 600,000 B. 1,200,000
   C. 1,800,000 D. 2,400,000
4. Today, there are _____, more than three times that number.
   A. 1,900,000 B. 3,760,000
   C. 5,670,000 D. 7,530,000

ROCKY MOUNTAIN ELK

5. In 1907, only about _____ elk could be counted in the U.S.
   A. 21,000 B. 41,000
   C. 101,000 D. 501,000

6. Today, populations in 10 western states total approximately _____.
   A. 100,000 B. 200,000
   C. 800,000 D. $1^1/_2$ million

WILD TURKEY

7. By the early 1900s, encroaching civilization and habitat loss may have reduced the wild turkey population to fewer than _____.
   A. 100,000 B. 200,000
   C. 500,000 D. 1 million
8. Today, conservation programs have restored the population to about _____ birds.
   A. 500,000 B. 1 million
   C. 3 million D. $4^1/_2$ million

PRONGHORN ANTELOPE

9. About 50 years ago, the total U.S. pronghorn population was only about _____.
   A. 12,000 B. 50,000
   C. 100,000 D. 500,000
10. Today, conservation programs have helped increase the population to more than _____.
    A. 250,000 B. 500,000
    C. 1 million D. 2 million

Answers: 1-A; 2-D; 3-B; 4-B; 5-B; 6-C; 7-A; 8-D; 9-A; 10-C

15

The Deer Hunter's Daypack

BY GREGG GUTSCHOW

E very deer hunter should carry a daypack on his back. A small backpack
is a critical piece of gear that helps
ensure that you'll have what you need
when you need it. And it's really the
only reasonable way to get all of your
gear out there comfortably and conve-
niently.

Invest in a good-sized pack with
wide shoulder straps and a waist belt.
You'll also want a daypack that is water-
resistant. Select a fleece backpack for
quietness. Also check out the zippers
before you buy. Find those that open
and close with a whisper. A topnotch
daypack is a solid investment that you'll
be happy to have.

PACKING YOUR PACK—THE NECESSITIES

Fire-starting kit. Whether it's waterproof matches, a butane lighter or some
other form of fire-starter, you'd better
have it.

Compass & map of the area. If
you are not *intimately* familiar with the
country, you must have a compass and
map and know how to use them.

Rope. Whether it's to pull your gun
or bow up into your treestand or to tie
branches together for an overnight shelter, 25 to 30 feet of thin rope is another
item you should always have.

Knife & sharpener. Best case scenario, you'll need it to field dress your
deer. Worst case, well, a knife comes in
handy for many jobs.

Safety harness. As soon as you get
in your treestand you must attach yourself securely, before you pull up the rest
of your gear or do anything else. Too
many people are killed or permanently
crippled every year in falls from treestands.

Headlamp & spare batteries.
Flashlights are fine, but the hands-free
utility of a headlamp is great when it
comes to finding your way into a stand
or blood-trailing a buck.

Optics. A hunter armed with good
optics sees more game and saves time

trying to assess whether or not the animal is one that he wants to shoot. And, especially when it comes to mature bucks, every second counts.

Pee bottle and toilet paper. Enough said.

NOT NECESSARY, BUT NICE

Snacks and drinking water. You won't hunt hard if you're not stocked up and well watered.

Multi-tool. One that could easily fall under the mandatory list.

Chemical handwarmers. Numb fingers don't do well when it comes to shooting a bow or working a safety on your deer rifle. If it's going to be colder than 40°F, have handwarmers.

Umbrella. You've probably seen the compact umbrellas that attach to the tree trunk above your stand.

Grunt calls, rattle box, deer lure. Depending on the hunting situation you may want any or all of these.

Wind detector. A small plastic puff bottle helps you check the air currents as the day progresses.

Camera. In-the-field photos of your deer are the best.

Unscented bow or gun lube. Nothing's worse than a squeaky tree-stand seat or an arrow rest that is suddenly making noise. Be prepared.

Screw-in bow hangers. Hang up rangefinder, binoculars, grunt call and the daypack itself.

Reflective tacks or flagging. If you shoot a deer and leave to get help to track it, you should use reflective tacks or surveyor's tape to mark the spot where you last saw the deer. Or you can use these items to mark a new scrape or rub that you want to check the next day. Clean up these items when you're done hunting.

Daypack Checklist

- ❏ Fire-starting kit
- ❏ Compass & map
- ❏ Rope
- ❏ Knife & sharpener
- ❏ Safety harness
- ❏ Headlamp & batteries
- ❏ Optics
- ❏ Pee bottle
- ❏ Snacks & water

- ❏ Multi-tool
- ❏ Chemical handwarmers
- ❏ Umbrella
- ❏ Grunt calls, rattle box, deer lure
- ❏ Wind detector
- ❏ Camera
- ❏ Unscented bow or gun lube
- ❏ Screw-in hangers
- ❏ Reflective tags or flagging

R E C I P E S

Recipes

Simple Goose Recipe

A young, tender wild goose may be prepared fairly quickly with this recipe.

Preparation

Place goose on rack in a shallow pan and roast in 400°F oven. Baste with butter and white or red wine. Roast for 35 to 45 minutes. Season with salt and pepper.

NRA Recipe

Did You know?

Did you know that sound waves can affect ballistics? Sound waves are defined as progressive longitudinal vibratory disturbances, says Venco Industries. The speed of sound varies slightly with air temperatures, but it's basically accepted that sound waves travel at 1,129 feet per second at 68°F.

"Bullets with very poor ballistic coefficients, like shotgun slugs, lose stability and, of course, accuracy when they go subsonic," says company spokesman Frank Ventimiglia. "That means when they slow to the point that they've dropped beneath the speed of sound, they are actually buffeted by the sound wave catching up to them from behind."

TIPS AFIELD

Treestand Benefits

When hunting for deer, do you station yourself on the ground? According to the National Bowhunter Education Foundation, there are good reasons for hunters, especially bowhunters, to consider elevating their position:

- Treestands offer the hunter a larger field of view.

- The hunter's scent is generally higher above the ground and disperses farther away from the immediate area. Scent dispersal is affected by eddies of the wind and other weather conditions.

- The hunter is above the animal's normal field of vision and can use this as an advantage by keeping visible movements to a minimum.

- A shot entering higher on the body of an animal and exiting nearer the bottom yields a better blood trail to aid in recovery.

- A hunter in a treestand is not moving about in the woods, reducing the possibility of interfering with another hunter.

- Because game shot from a treestand often travels less distance after being shot, the result is a shorter blood trail.

Treestands allow for a better view of nongame wildlife, adding to the enjoyment of the total hunting experience.

BEFORE YOU GO

*J*ust as you pack the right gear to help ensure a successful outing, so must you be prepared as a driver to handle the challenging terrain you may encounter, with a sensitivity toward preserving the environment. So Chevy Truck suggests that before you get behind the wheel, consider the following driving checklist:

- What are the local laws for operating a truck off road? Is any special equipment or a license for the driver or the vehicle needed? If unsure, check with the park ranger's office or a local law enforcement agency.

- How difficult are the roads and trails in the area you have chosen? Do all of the drivers in your group possess the skills needed to handle these trails?

- Is the vehicle's spare tire fully inflated and ready for use?

Proper tire pressure is listed on the sidewall.

- Is the vehicle well maintained? Excessive emissions, leaking fuel and dripping oil may not only cause you problems but also pollute the environment.

- If traveling to a remote area, take extra time for planning. Know the terrain and plan your route. Get accurate trail maps and try to learn of any blocked or closed roads. It's a good idea to advise the park ranger when you will be traveling in remote areas; or travel with another vehicle for added safety.

- Plan ahead and make sure your vehicle is off-road ready.

SOMETHING TO SHOOT FOR

WHITE-TAILED DEER

HUNTER:
Rachel Jordan

RESIDENCE:
Dodgeville, WI

WHERE TAKEN:
Dodgeville, Wisconsin

ARMS USED:
Browning .300 Mag, Win Action
Rifle; 165-Grain Hornady Bullets

Rachel was hunting the family farm when this monster came into view.

HUNTER:
Nick Brantner

RESIDENCE:
Rothschild, WI

WHERE TAKEN:
Central Iowa

ARMS USED:
Mathews MQ1 Bow

Hunting Geese & Ducks in Northern Ontario
BY GLENN SAPIR

"*Nika! Nika!*" Adam Suganaqueb excitedly whispered as he pointed toward the western horizon.

The old man could not see the birds. His broken eyeglasses sat in a drawer in his home at the Webequie Settlement. It would be another month or two before the circuit eye doctor made his periodic visit to the native settlement in northern Ontario. So Adam strained his fine-tuned ears to compensate for his impaired vision.

The call of the Canadas, imperceptible to me when Adam first signalled, now became louder as the birds drew closer to their morning feeding area to our south.

Hunkered down in our willow blind on the southern tip of an island in Ontario's Winisk River, Adam began to call. For some of the geese in this flock, their education in hunting was about to commence; many were birds of the year, and this bog-rich country is where their lives had begun only a few months before.

"We-onk, We-onk, WE-ONK, WE-ONK," barked tantalizingly from Adam's mouth. Soon similar sounds rang out 10 yards away, where Mathias Suganaqueb kneeled with hunter Butch Furtman at the other end of the blind.

The geese, still quite high, indecisively began to circle over the few plastic feeding-goose decoys staked at the water's rocky edge where emergent weeds offered attractive feed.

The two men continued to call, but the geese gave no indication they would alight at this nonscheduled stop.

Mathias snapped orders in Ojibway to Randy Suganaqueb to begin calling too. Randy, until then, had lain flat on his back, not moving or uttering a sound.

The enticement of this new, high-pitched call, added to the loud, deeper sounds from Adam and Mathias—all made without the aid of an artificial device—excitedly delivered an invitation that the circling geese couldn't refuse. They lowered their altitude and circled for their final approach, dropping their legs and cupping their wings. When they were only 10 feet above the water and within fair range of our 12 gauges and 2³/₄-inch magnum 2s, we four men revealed our presence. Furtman and I took the first shots, soon followed by the booming of Mathias's and Adam's shotguns.

In the shallow water lay five dead Canada geese.

For centuries, the natives of the Winisk River region of northern Ontario have lived off the land. Both Cree and Ojibway have hunted moose, caribou and black bear. Willow ptarmigan, in their white seasonal plumage, range into the area in winter, and ruffed grouse, truly "fool's hens" here, as well as sharptail grouse, are plentiful.

Varying hares have fallen to Ojibway snares and guns. In their nets the natives have taken walleyes, northern pike, brook trout, whitefish and sturgeon.

And, of course, there are waterfowl!

Hundreds of thousands of geese and ducks nest in this area. Rivers, often slowing down between rapids to form giant lakes, dominate the region.

Among the soft-padded muskeg, countless bogs recede at a snail's pace, as they have since the melting glaciers of the ice age created them.

Now the Ojibway of Webequie Settlement live off the fish and game in an additional way. They have established hunting and fishing camps, owned, operated and guided by their own people. Butch Furtman of Duluth, Minnesota, and I would spend a few days in mid-September at their goose camp. We were to enjoy gunning opportunities in a remarkable region and gain an insight to the land and its people through three generations of Ojibway hunters, perhaps representing the past, present and future.

Continued ...

with an oxbow lake. The waterfowl had been trading between the two bodies of water, and the channel seemed to be a marker for a well-traveled flight path. We were all intently scanning the skies when we were surprised to hear quacking off to our left. When we slowly turned our heads, we could see a flock of greenwing teal swimming in the channel 100 yards upstream.

Adam, without a word, got on his hands and knees and quietly skulked through the thick, five-foot-high scrub brush and willows. Soon he was 25 yards away from us, calling like a duck, using only his voice.

Mathias whispered to us, "My father has lured in swimming ducks by rustling the high weeds and brush along the shore. He's even waved a white handkerchief just above the weeds to make the ducks curious."

Then Mathias crawled toward his father. Soon, the rustling of the weeds began again, though we could barely hear the commotion. The next sounds were far more audible. Mathias unloaded his gun on the swimming flock. Five teal lay dead in the water.

Adam Suganaqueb, born in this wilderness, was orphaned at a young age. With no father to teach him the ways of survival, it fell upon his older brother to foster Adam's skills in fishing and hunting. Different families, Ojibway and Cree, took them in throughout their childhood years.

"We live in settlement," Adam related to me in his limited English. "We travel where there's fish and game."

He grew up something of a nomad, following the trails where bountiful game led him, and when we were together, he was enjoying his 80th year and still imparting knowledge onto his progeny ...

It was morning, and the three Suganaquebs, Furtman and I sat in a blind overlooking a channel that connected the main body of the Winisk

Mathias Suganaqueb, age 37 at the time, had been taught much of the old ways by his father. The idea was to kill the game for food. It mattered not whether they were swimming or flying. But unlike his father, he also learned much of the new ways of the world. He went to school in Webequie, then a settlement of 500 people. Next he lived in Thunder Bay, a modern city in southern Ontario on the northern shore of Lake Superior, where he attended public schools through the 12th grade. Since then, occasional college seminars have increased his formal education.

Mathias was a partner in Winisk Wilderness Camps, and with that title came much of the administrative responsibilities involved in running such an operation. His desk in Webequie was covered by ledgers, files and papers that showed he was entrenched in managerial duties.

Mathias, however, was still very much part of the old tradition. In winter he tended his trapline; in spring he prepared for the fishing season; in summer he fished and guided; in fall he guided the waterfowlers, using the knowledge he learned from Adam, who first began taking him on hunts when he was 13. Mathias too talks like the birds, and he's gained the confidence needed to direct a hunt, even when his father is along ...

It was September 14, late afternoon, when Furtman (filming a special for his television audience in the upper Midwest and southern Ontario) and I hunkered down in the blind on the southern end of the island we were to fire from the next day.

Mathias had urged us to bring our shotguns, but that afternoon, the eve of the earliest waterfowl hunting season opener I've ever participated in, we were going to shoot with our cameras.

Mathias took charge. First he instructed his 11-year-old son Randy where to place the decoys, and when Randy returned to the blind, Mathias told him where to lie—quietly and motionlessly.

Adam positioned himself 10 yards away. The first flight of geese came out of the western sky, and when it became clear the birds might come our way, Mathias quickly planned his strategy, giving his father orders in his native, guttural Ojibway language, an Algonquin dialect.

"There are geese to the west," is the translation of the first message from Mathias to his father. "You call first, then I'll join. NOW, call!"

Adam followed his son's directions.

"We-onk, we-onk, we-onk, we-onk."

Mathias joined in.

"We-onk, we-onk, we-onk."

Together father and son harmonized, and the geese came in for a better look. Furtman and I took our shots—with our cameras.

Continued ...

25

For as long as sportsmen have come to the Winisk, whose waters flow northeastward to Hudson Bay, the Ojibway have served as guides. Mathias was first permitted to accompany his father on a guided trip when he was 13, and he himself was allowed to guide the next year. The trip when he was 13 was unforgettable.

"Photographers wished to canoe all the way down the Winisk to Hudson Bay," Mathias recalled. "I came along to translate for my father and these men. We fished and hunted for much of our food. We took the whole summer. I went to places I had never been to before or since."

On my hunt, Randy Suganaqueb, Mathias's 11-year-old son, was making his first outing accompanying his father while he was guiding. At the same time, Randy's cousin Dale was in moose camp with Mathias's brother. School would have to be sacrificed for a week. So is the way of education of the Ojibway hunters and fishermen.

Each day in the blind Randy would find an out-of-the-way spot for his small body. He'd volunteer no words, and he'd answer all questions with Gary Cooperesque one-syllable replies. His school in Webequie conducted classes in English, so it wasn't the language barrier that prevented communication.

If he didn't talk, however, he certainly listened. He placed the decoys where his father ordered; he would *gidahay nika*—call the geese—when his father so instructed him in Ojibway.

When whistling sandhill cranes, protected from non-Native hunters by law, flew by, far out of range, Randy alone persisted in calling them. His calls duplicated the cranes' whistling, and after a few minutes of persistent mimicking, he finally lured back the birds. His father readied his shotgun, and at a distance that made shooting a calculated gamble, Mathias sprung up and fired. This time Mathias missed. Adam laughed loudly at his son's futile attempt, and Randy simply resumed his silence and reposed posture.

By the James Bay Treaty, or Treaty No. 9, of 1905, and the "adhesion" in 1930, the Ojibway of this region were given exemption from fish and game laws. As Mathias paraphrased it, "We retain our old hunting, fishing and trapping rights for as long as the sun shines and the river flows—and all that stuff."

Later, Mathias told me he had no grand plan for Randy's future, though one of his sons was presently living and studying in Thunder Bay. It was apparent, however, that whatever path Randy traveled, he would bring with him a knowledge of hunting, a tradition passed on by his father and father's father.

Canada Goose
BRANTA CANADENSIS

OTHER NAMES:

Goose, Canadian, Canada, honker

CHARACTERISTICS:

Our largest goose, the Canada is easily recognizable by its size and its bright white cheek-throat patch. Males and females look alike with a black head and neck, the white cheek-throat patch mentioned, and brownish-gray back, wings and sides. There are more than a dozen subspecies.

HABITAT:

In the far North, tundra makes excellent breeding habitat. In the Lower 48, marshlands, lakeshores and backwaters support plenty of geese. When grain is in the agricultural fields—either short grain on the stalk or spillage amongst the stubble after harvesting, geese will travel back and forth between the food source and their water resting grounds.

FOOD:

Small grains are important when available. Grasses, clover, alfalfa, winter wheat and other greens are also preferred.

BEHAVIOR:

Morning and late afternoon are prime feeding times. Geese will rest on water between times.

NESTING:

Islands, the top of a muskrat house or beaver dam, a hummock of bulrushes, man-made breeding platforms. It is true that a pair of geese will mate for life; but if one dies, the other will take a new mate.

HUNTING STRATEGIES:

There are three good ways to hunt sharp-eyed and wary Canada geese. One: Set up decoys in a feeding field before first light or in the early afternoon, then hide well, and well within range of the decoys, and call to the incoming geese to lure them to your setup. Two: Try to pass-shoot geese traveling corridors between feeding areas and resting waters; this is tough. Finally: Use decoys on the water to try to tempt geese returning from feeding. One more important point: Use enough gun—12 gauge minimum, 3-inch shells (magnum preferred), large shot—and don't shoot at birds more than 30 or so yards away. These birds are BIG and TOUGH, and it's mighty easy to wing one and never see it again. Be responsible.

—Tom Carpenter

MULE DEER

HUNTER:
Randy Kutskill

RESIDENCE:
Sterling Heights, MI

WHERE TAKEN:
Northwest Wyoming

ARMS USED:
Ruger 7mm Remington
Mag Rifle

Randy, above, and his guide Don Daems

HUNTER:
George Vamos

RESIDENCE:
Mountain Top, PA

WHERE TAKEN:
Montana

ARMS USED:
.300 Winchester Mag Rifle;
Browning Stainless Stalker

TIPS AFIELD

Treestand Maintenance: It's Essential

No hunter should ever use any treestand without thoroughly inspecting it for defects, missing parts or weaknesses, reports the National Bowhunters Education Foundation. Be sure all bolts are tightened, and frayed ropes, straps and worn chains are replaced before placing the stand in the tree. Here are other tips for preparing your treestand:

- Camo paint the treestand and steps to reduce the shiny metal and new-wood glare that can spook your quarry. Do this two or three months before using the stand to give it time for the new-paint smell to fade. Use dull colors in brown, black, gray or tan for best results.

- Metal and wood tend to squeak or groan. You should test your stand before the hunting season to eliminate the potential for noises.

- You can use vegetable oil as a lubricant on stands. It's odorless! Carry a small vial in your pack for touch-ups in the field.

- Some treestand manufacturers offer an adhesive-backed, coarse grid strip to apply to the stand's surface to help improve traction. This is particularly useful on solid wood platforms or on those that do not have an open grid design.

- Dip new chains in liquid rubber, available at most hardware stores. This will quiet the stand and hide shine. Several thin coats of black or brown work best. Apply by dipping, hanging to dry and dipping again. Take care that the links do not glue themselves together while drying.

- If you choose to leave your stand in place rather than remove it after each hunt, secure your stand with a padlock and chain.

- When leaving your stand out in foul weather, place a piece of plastic over the top of the platform and lash it down with an elastic shock cord. This will keep it clean and dry.

- Dye white or bright-colored ropes and straps a drab color to help camouflage them. Painting usually makes them stiff and hard to use.

I've Fallen and I Can't Get Up

A fall from a treestand can be tragic. Do whatever you can to minimize the serious ramifications of such an event, as advised by the National Bowhunters Education Foundation.

- Be equipped with basic safety and survival items. Carry a whistle, a plastic survival blanket—or, at the least, a plastic garbage bag with holes cut out for head and arms—an Ace bandage, a roll of adhesive tape, matches in a waterproof container, knife, fire-starter, water bottle, compass, map, flashlight and extra batteries, two bandannas and survival food, such as granola.

- Before you go on the hunt, leave word with a responsible person, informing him or her of exactly where you plan to hunt.

- Hunt with a companion. Arrange whistle signals for each other and leave a location note with the vehicle. Set a time with your partner or, if you're hunting alone, with another responsible person for your return, as well as a plan of action to follow if the hunter is late.

- If you fall, adopt a deliberate plan of action: S.T.O.P.–Stop, Think, Observe, Plan.

- Use what is available. Clothing or bandannas, for example, can serve for padding, warmth and bandages. Belts, shoelaces, bowstring or hauling line can secure splints and even be used to make a stretcher. Bows, arrows, branches or poles can offer rigid support for fractures and severe sprains.

- Remember your **ABCs**: Clear and maintain Airway; restore and maintain Breathing; restore and maintain Circulation.

- Don't panic. Fight the urge by knowing what to do, when and how. Before the hunting season, consider taking a Red Cross basic First Aid course. You will gain both knowledge and confidence.

- Check for spinal injury. If a spinal or other serious injury is suspected, restrict movement until emergency personnel arrive.

- Prevent shock. Conserve body heat by covering body with any extra clothing available.

- Check for broken bones.

- Use signals. Three blasts on a whistle may summon help if nearby. A fire by night or a smoky fire by day gives warmth and also serves as a location signal for rescuers.

Recipes

Baked Doves

Doves are an ammunition manufacturer's dream game bird: More ammo is expended on doves, in fact, than any other game animal. Once you get your doves, you'll want to make the most of them, and here is one way:

Ingredients

8 to 10 doves
Flour, salt and pepper
6 tbsp. butter, divided
2 tbsp. flour

$^2/_3$ cup canned chicken
   broth or stock
1 tsp. Worcestershire sauce
1 tsp. onion juice

Preparation

Dust doves with seasoned flour. Melt 4 tablespoons butter in a skillet. Place doves, breast side down, in skillet and brown on both sides. Remove doves from skillet and place in a deep casserole. Melt two more tbsp. butter in skillet and stir in 2 tbsp. flour. Add chicken broth gradually, stirring constantly. Cook for a few minutes and then stir in Worcestershire sauce and onion juice. Salt and pepper this gravy to taste. Pour gravy over doves, cover casserole and bake in a preheated 325°F oven for about 1 hour or until tender. Baste frequently with sauce, adding more broth if needed.

NRA Recipe

Dram: Old Measurement Still Used

T he current labeling system for shotgun shells came into being years ago when shotgun shells were loaded with black powder, reports Joe Ventimiglia. For instance, a box labeled "3¹/₄—1¹/₈—8" contained shells loaded with 3¹/₄ drams of blackpowder and 1¹/₈ ounce of No. 8 shot. Blackpowder is now obsolete, yet the labeling process remains.

"Today, shot shells are loaded with smokeless powder, and boxes are marked to show what a given charge is equivalent to in the old blackpowder dram rating," explains Ventimiglia. "Shooters still use it to evaluate the effectiveness of a specific load."

"But remember, smokeless powder is measured in grains and a very small amount is equal to a much heavier charge of blackpowder. To load a shell with 3¹/₄ drams of smokeless powder would be catastrophic."

• HELP Yourself •

W aterfowlers run the deadly risk of capsizing their hunting craft. Do you know what to do if it happens to you? Here is a suggestion from the National Rifle Association.

If you fall into the water wearing a personal flotation device and can't get to shore or back in the boat, you can delay hypothermia by assuming the **Heat Escape Lessening Position (HELP)**. Cross your ankles, place your arms across your chest, draw your knees into your abdomen and lean back. This lessens the loss of body heat in cold water by 50 percent. Two or more persons should assume the huddle position by placing their arms around each other and maintaining chest-to-chest contact.

TIPS AFIELD

Field Dressing Tips

Your first job once you've recovered downed game is to tag it. Your second is to field-dress it. Here are field dressing tips from the National Bowhunters Education Foundation:

1 Roll the animal onto its back.

2 With a sharp knife tip, cut around the anal opening to free the end of the intestines from the skin. Start at the sternum, or breastbone, cut carefully toward the pelvis, through the skin and thin wall of the body cavity. Be careful not to cut the intestines or you will contaminate the meat.

3 Once the body cavity is opened, roll the animal on its side so gravity will help remove viscera. With most of the viscera free from the body, now it is time for you to carefully cut the tissues connecting the viscera along the backbone. If the end of the intestine was properly freed, it should easily pull away from the pelvis area.

4 Once the viscera is free, cut around the edges of the diaphragm, a thin, flat muscle that separates the lung area from the viscera. This exposes the heart and lungs. Reach forward and cut through the esophagus and windpipe at the front end of the rib cage and remove the lungs and heart.

5 Turn the animal on its belly with the head elevated as much as possible to drain any accumulated blood. As soon as possible, wash off the interior of the body cavity with water to remove blood, dirt and hair. Then wipe the interior of the body cavity thoroughly dry with a cloth, paper towels or dried grass.

MORE TIPS

- Smaller animals can be hung up with hauling line for easier field dressing. Large animals can be skinned and quartered for easier transport. Check local laws regarding rules on transporting game.

- In warm climates, game should be skinned as soon as possible. Pepper sprinkled on meat will discourage flies. A body net will also protect the meat from flies.

WHITE-TAILED DEER

HUNTER:
William Peklay

RESIDENCE:
Madison, OH

WHERE TAKEN:
Northern Ohio

ARMS USED:
Bow

HUNTER:
John Neal

RESIDENCE:
Kingston, MA

WHERE TAKEN:
Ohio

ARMS USED:
Martin Bow;
85-Grain Thunderhead Gold
Tip Arrow

Turkey Vest Checklist

Chris Kirby, renowned turkey hunter, calls the turkey vest a "portable filing cabinet." Here are his suggestions of items you may want to stow in yours. We've left blank lines for you to add items. Make a copy of this and use it season after season to make sure you have the items you need.

- ❏ Small flashlight
- ❏ Folding saw or pruning shears
- ❏ Knife
- ❏ Utility tool
- ❏ Compass
- ❏ Cough drops
- ❏ Insect repellant
- ❏ Compact binoculars
- ❏ Decoy(s) and stake(s)
- ❏ Mouth diaphragm calls
- ❏ Box call
- ❏ One-handed box call
- ❏ Slate, aluminum and/or glass call
- ❏ Striker(s) for the above call(s)
- ❏ Call maintenance kit (sandpaper, chalk, small plastic bag)
- ❏ Locator calls
- ❏ Drink (soft-pouched or plastic bottle)
- ❏ Energy snack

- ❏ Toilet paper in a zip-top plastic bag
- ❏ Raingear
- ❏ Shotgun shells
- ❏ Pen
- ❏ String or wire ties
- ❏ Surveyor tape
- ❏ Pocket-sized camera
- ❏ First-aid kit
- ❏ Face mask
- ❏ Gloves
- ❏ Seat cushion
- ❏ Waterproof matches and/or cigarette lighter
- ❏ Space blanket
- ❏ GPS
- ❏ Hand warmers
- ❏ _____
- ❏ _____
- ❏ _____

A Boy's First Hunt

BY GLENN SAPIR

*I*t's easy to pin down some of my life's highlights. Getting married, watching the birth of my daughter and bringing my newborn son home from the hospital are a few. Now I can add a Saturday in November.

The story begins with the opening of New York's deer hunting season on a Monday. I watched for deer on a wooded hillside in central Putnam County in southern New York that morning. Shots at any of five does presented themselves, but I had reserved the opener for a buck.

Later that day, I hunted for three more hours until legal shooting time ended. When I returned to my Putnam home, my eight-year-old son eagerly met me at the door.

"Did you get one?" Mark asked, hazel eyes opened wide and focused on my own tired and not nearly so wide-open peepers.

"Nope," was my succinct reply.

He turned his back and walked away dejected. Apparently, I'd let him down.

Tuesday was no better. In fact, I never even saw a tail, and by now I was ready to fill my antlerless deer tag. Predictably, Mark was at the downstairs entrance as the groaning of the electric garage door signalled my return.

"Did you get one?" he queried, like a broken record.

"Didn't even see one," I shrugged.

Mark scowled, then turned without a sound.

By Friday, the end-of-the-day scene was getting old.

"Dad, I'm going out with you tomorrow."

From an eight-year-old, that should have been a question, instead of an order.

We didn't talk about it again until after dinner, when my son asked, "What time should I set my alarm clock for?"

"Forget it," was my less than tactful reply.

A torrent of tears was his.

"Okay, okay," I relented. "We'll hunt in the afternoon. You won't have to wake up as early, it won't be as cold, and we won't be out as long."

With shirt cuffs drying each eye, Mark nodded as he accepted the compromise. Less noticeably, I wrote off any chance of success for our scheduled hunt.

Typically, I'll be in the woods by 2 o'clock for my afternoon session. That day, I did all I could to delay our start. But by 3 p.m., Mark wasn't to be denied.

Mark proudly slipped my orange hunting vest over the several layers of clothing I'd insisted he wear. Atop his head was one of my orange hunting caps.

Soon, we were ready. Before we set out for our ground stand, I told Mark some rules. Silence and stillness were crucial; he had never before shown signs of mastering either.

"Once we enter the woods, no talking. If I see a deer, I'll whisper it to you, and you must be perfectly still."

Then I loaded my 12 gauge pump shotgun with five slugs.

Mark followed my every step, the bottom of the orange vest dragging along the ground, the hat covering him down to his eyebrows.

We were soon on a large boulder that I used as my ground stand. Twenty minutes later, despite all odds, I saw movement in the thick woods perhaps 70 yards away.

"There's a deer," I whispered, and Mark immediately put a finger in each ear.

I raised my shotgun, steadied my aim against a tree, and looked through my 2-power scope for a sight picture. Only one spot in the thick timber might present a clean shot at a vital area if one of the two feeding white-

tails that I thought I saw would position itself just right.

After what seemed an eternity, but may have been two minutes, a deer's side appeared in my crosshairs. I squeezed the trigger, Mark jumped, and the two deer ran off.

"I must have missed," I sighed though I thought I had seen something fall after the shot. "Well, anyway, you saw something exciting," I continued.

Mark smiled. "It was really exciting, Dad."

"Let's just wait a minute," I told him. Then he followed me toward the spot the deer had been.

Continued ...

As I approached that spot, dejection was flooded out by exhilaration. I waved for Mark to join me, where on the ground lay a huge doe, dead.

We hugged and slapped high fives, then I started to dig into my backpack for plastic gloves, a bag and a drag. At the same time, Mark studied the deer as its brown eyes glazed into postmortem blue.

"Dad, you know, I'm kind of sad," Mark said, lifting his eyes from the deer's to mine.

"I am, too, Mark," I said with the emotion I truly felt. "I'm always sad when I kill an animal, but I'm also very proud, and I'm happy that you were with me when we did it."

With those words, Mark's face lit up. When the field dressing was done, and the drag out of the woods was about to begin, Mark volunteered to do the work. One yank on the drag pulled him back toward the deer.

"You better do it, Dad."

As we walked out, Mark led the way, excitedly warning me of any obstructions that lay ahead.

When we got the deer out of the woods, I kneeled down to look at the doe again. Mark put his small hand on my shoulder and said, "I'm your lucky charm."

He was that day—and I hope he will be on many hunts to come.

• The Right Cleaning Rod •

The best cleaning rods consist of one piece. Jointed rods have more flexibility, but the joints provide potential areas to collect embedded particles or sharp edges that can harm barrels. There are two schools of thought concerning the design of one-piece rods: some shooters like hardened steel rods, while others prefer plastic-coated rods. The theory is that a hard steel rod will not embed grit and become a "file." Other shooters prefer a coated rod because they believe that as a rod flexes inside the bore, it continuously hits the lands of the rifling. The theory is that a steel rod will continuously hit the barrel at the flex point and "peen" the rifling as it pushes the patch through, while a coated rod provides some protection against that. For what it's worth, most serious shooters I know use coated rods.

— Bryce Towsley

MULE DEER

HUNTER:
John Pellissier

RESIDENCE:
Klamath Falls, OR

WHERE TAKEN: Oregon

ARMS USED:
7mm Ruger; Remington 150-Grain
Bullets

HUNTER:
Gregory Orlowski

RESIDENCE:
Amherst, WI

WHERE TAKEN:
Gateway, Colorado

ARMS USED:
.30-06 Rifle

TIPS AFIELD

Turkey Hunter's Responsibilites

The National Rifle Association reports that, according to hunter education experts, the leading cause of turkey hunting accidents is a hunter being mistaken for game. Here are tips on how to act responsibly while turkey hunting:

- Positively identify your target. Use binoculars to ensure that what you see is a turkey. Never substitute a scope for binoculars.

- Don't shoot at what you think is a "piece of a turkey." You must see the whole bird before you can determine whether it is legal and safe to shoot.

- Don't shoot at movement or sounds.

- Don't stalk turkey sounds or try to sneak in for a shot.

- Where rifles or handguns are legal, be especially careful of the target's long-range background.

- Don't use a headnet that obscures your vision.

What's in a Name ?

The .30-30 and the .30-06 may well be the two most popular rifle calibers in American history. Do you know how these venerable loads got their names?

Both are .30 caliber bullets. The .30-30 was a 30 WCF (Winchester Center Fire) that was originally loaded with 30 grains of smokeless powder just as the .30-40 Krag was a .30 caliber Army round loaded with 40 grains. Neither load today necessarily digests the same powder charge weights that these numbers once signified.

"The .30-06 was a .30 caliber military round that actually originated in 1903 as a 220-grain bullet," describes champion shooter Joe Ventimiglia. "But in 1906 it was modified to better handle a more efficient 150-grain bullet, and the year of that modification was used so that people would know the difference. The Army listing was 'ball cartridge, caliber 30, Model of 1906.'"

Other rifle and pistol cartridges are named for their diameters, but those numbers aren't necessarily exact, either, comments Ventimiglia.

Wild Turkey

MELEAGRIS GALLOPOVO

OTHER NAMES:

Turkey, gobbler

CHARACTERISTICS:

Our largest gamebird, a full-grown tom (male or gobbler) will easily go 20 pounds; in some areas of the midwest, you might find a 25-, 28- or even 30-pounder! Hens will go 10 to 12 pounds. Five subspecies exist—the Eastern, Osceola or Florida, the Rio Grande, the Merriam's and Gould's. Little description is needed for these all-American originals! Gobblers have huge tail fans, a "beard" protruding from the chest, a blue-and-white head in spring, and sharp spurs for fighting. Hens are drab brown.

HABITAT:

Wild turkeys were once thought to need vast expanses of unbroken, mature hardwoods. But we now know that isn't true. Agricultural areas with only 20 percent woods now hold turkeys, and Western species like the Rio Grande and Merriam's have always existed in places where trees are in somewhat short supply. Basic needs are a few trees for roosting, feed, a good water source, and some cover to escape to.

FOOD:

Wild turkeys feed on what's available and are very adaptable and opportunistic. Start the list with fruits, nuts, acorns, seeds, grains, grass shoots and roots ...

and try to finish it with insects, small frogs and toads, even lizards. Turkeys will feed in the early morning and evening.

BEHAVIOR:

Turkeys roost in trees, up and out of night predators' way, and come down to feed in the morning. There's another feeding session in the evening. In between, they wll loaf in good cover. Gobblers will stick together, as will hens and young birds.

NESTING:

There are few sights like a strutting, spitting, drumming gobbler, doing all he can to impress and lure in a hen for mating. He will also gobble mightily to make his presence known far and wide. Once the relationship is consummated, the hen goes off to nest (8 to 15 brown-speckled eggs) and raise the poults once they hatch.

HUNTING STRAGETIES:

In spring: Dress in camouflage head to toe—that includes your face and socks and hands—and set up comfortably at the base of a big tree, within a couple hundred yards of a gobbler. Use a call (practice a lot before the season) and sound like a hen to lure the amorous gobbler into shotgun range. Easier said than done! In fall: Scatter a flock far and wide, then set up and try to call them back together.   —Tom Carpenter

ALL IN FUN

HUNTING HUMOR

Tomasic art

"Dog-gone this new high-tech camo!
I laid my jacket down, and now I can't find it!"

Muzzleloader Elk

BY SCOTT SEVERSON

The day my Colorado muzzle-loader elk tag arrived was the beginning of my elk hunting experience, even though the season was months away. I spent my summer thinking and reading about elk. I watched videos about elk and elk hunting. I studied catalogs for gear that would aid me on my quest. I spent hours shooting my muzzleloader, experimenting with different charges and bullets until I found a suitable combination.

September finally arrived, and I was ready. In two weeks I would leave for Colorado. I had enough gear to equip two hunters. My rifle was sighted in, and I was confident in my skill with it. I had thoroughly annoyed my wife and dogs by practicing my elk bugle and cow calls. I had even worked in a horseback-riding lesson over the summer.

The day of our departure arrived. Dad, Terry, Dave and I began the long journey from Minnesota to northwestern Colorado in my 4WD and Terry's pickup truck. After 2 days of driving, we reached our hotel in Colorado. The next morning we would pack in.

We got up early, drove to the outfitter's place and had breakfast. There's nothing like a huge, greasy breakfast

just before you're going to be bounced around on a horse for the next several hours.

After breakfast we drove to the trailhead to pick up our horses and pack in. Two cowboys met us there. I decided to ride my horse a little to get to know her before attempting to lead the pack team into the mountains. I mounted a bay and paused to take in the intoxicating scent of saddle leather and horse, blended with clean mountain air. I gave the horse a little nudge with my heel so that we could trot a little before hitting the trail. Instead, we went from standing still to a full-blast gallop in a second! After I got over the fear of falling off and being trampled to death, the ride became quite enjoyable. I was really feeling like a cowboy.

Not 10 minutes on the trail, Terry's horse slipped and then righted itself, thoroughly coating me with mud. The trail, which paralleled a beautiful stream that flowed down the mountain, was extremely muddy due to recent rains and ran uphill all the way. It was slow going. After about 3 hours we made it to base camp. Our camp overlooked a beautiful valley, where a crystal-clear stream snaked through the valley floor. After unloading our gear, Dave and I turned around to return the horses. Leaving the horses, we gathered the packs and rifles that we hadn't had room for on the first trip and began a 6-mile hike back to base camp. About 20 minutes into the uphill hike in the thin mountain air, I began to hear voices from earlier that summer. "Scott, have you started working out for your elk hunt?" co-workers asked. "Work out? I'm in fine shape," I answered. Now I was 3 miles in, 3 miles yet to go, and the 40-pound pack felt more like 400. Dave and I didn't talk much; we were trying to conserve oxygen. We finally crested the hill that revealed our tents in the valley below, but before we got to camp I swore an oath that all out-of-shape elk hunters pledge: Next elk

hunting trip I'm going to be in better shape.

Dad and Terry had set up camp while Dave and I were gone. Our camp consisted of two two-man tents for sleeping, a small storage tent for our gear and a lean-to for cooking. I was exhausted and exhilarated at the same time. I inhaled my meal of freeze-dried turkey tetrazzini and shortly thereafter retired to my tent. I lay awake listening to the haunting bugles of elk, thinking that life can't get much better than this. A storm rolled through, and the rain against my tent and cry of bugling elk lulled me to sleep.

Morning came, and my spirits were high, even if my back and legs were

Continued ...

The author, above, with his dad and their muzzleloader elk.

The author, above, as he leads the packstring into base camp in Colorado.

complaining. Today we were going to scout for elk sign to determine where we would hunt tomorrow. Dad and I went in one direction, and Terry and Dave went in the other. Since Dad had hunted this area before, I followed him. We hiked for hours, looking for fresh elk sign. As I silently followed Dad through the mountains, I was reminded of the many times he brought me hunting as a boy ...

Dad first started taking me along on squirrel hunts in a neighbor's woods. I was too young to carry a gun, so I would follow, carrying a stick. As I grew older he brought me along on hunts for geese, ducks, pheasant and deer. My best times with Dad have always been hunting. He taught me what it means to be a safe and ethical hunter; he bought me my first hunting dog; and, most importantly, he always seemed to like having me along.

After an unsuccessful morning of scouting, we hiked back to camp for lunch. After lunch, Dad and I scouted some more. We were trying to locate an area that he had heard about from a friend, and after a little scouting, we found the switchbacks Dad's friend had told him about. We followed them to a park that had fresh elk sign, and we decided I would overlook that park on opening day. Dad found a spot a few hundred yards away.

Back at camp, anticipation was running high. Sleep didn't come easy that night. Dad and I were awake before the alarm went off at 5 a.m. It rained again during the night, and most of our gear was wet by now. We took turns getting dressed in the small tent, because there was only room for one person to move at a time. After a quick breakfast and an inspection of my muzzleloader, we were off.

Things always seem to take longer in the dark. It seemed as if I had hiked for miles before I finally got to the park where I would sit for the morning. I settled in and said a quick prayer that my muzzleloader would go off if I got a shot. It was a beautiful morning, with a light mist in the air. Just before light, I started to hear bugling from the mountain just east of me. Just being in elk country is exciting, but when you hear bugling, it really quickens your pulse. I bugled back and forth with it for about half an hour before it stopped.

A couple of hours passed when, like an apparition, a large cow elk sauntered into the park. My heart pounded. I had a cow tag. Should I take her, I asked myself, or wait for a bull? After watching her a little longer to make sure she didn't have a calf with her, I decided to take a shot. I slowly raised my muzzleloader, pulled back the hammer and

cocked the set trigger. I had a 60-yard broadside shot; it wouldn't get any better than this. As I placed my sight behind the cow's front shoulder I thought my heart was literally going to leap from my chest. I held my breath and squeezed the trigger. The rifle let out a thunderous boom. After the smoke cleared, I saw the elk lying with its hooves in the air. I quickly began to reload. When I finished, I looked in the direction of the elk; it was standing! I fired; again the elk went down. Once again I reloaded, then walked over to the downed animal. Two shots had caused mortal wounds. I finished her, however, with a shot to the neck.

I gave thanks for my elk, and in my excitement I let out a holler. As Dad says, "If you don't get a little excited, you shouldn't be out here."

We hunted another 3 days, but my cow was the only elk taken. Though we didn't take any "trophies" on this trip, it was an experience I'll never forget. I had a rare opportunity to hunt elk and ride horses in some of the most beautiful country I have ever seen. I took my first elk with a muzzleloading rifle, and I have another great memory of hunting with my dad. For me, at least, this hunt was one for the record books.

TIPS AFIELD

Rifle Scope Pointers

BY GLENN SAPIR

When comparing rifle scopes, hunters tend to favor models that allow pinpoint aiming at targets hundreds of yards away, accuracy in low-light conditions and improved visibility in brushy terrain. Most hunters, however, tend to overlook the fact that a rifle scope must conform to their personal needs if a hunt is to be successful. By taking the time to understand fully the dynamics of a rifle scope, a hunter can make a long-term investment that will bring satisfying results. Here are suggestions offered by Carl Zeiss Optical, Inc., manufacturer of fine sporting optics.

First, identify the numbers that correspond to power (magnification) and the diameter of the objective lens. Generally, larger objective lenses allow more light into the system, increasing optical performance. A higher magnification decreases optical performance, especially the field of view and resolution. So, a higher magnification coupled with a smaller objective decreases the exit pupil, an asset in low-light viewing. A rule of thumb is that doubling the power decreases light and resolution by one-half.

A common mistake among inexperienced hunters is to select a rifle scope with excessive magnification. This may create obstacles when shooting at close range. Because safety and success depend on a wide field of view, a low-power rifle scope is recommended. This prevents the firearm from moving as the target advances.

Use a **high-power** rifle scope for hunting in the West or other places where you will be shooting across open terrain. Long-range shooting requires high magnification for accuracy and visibility. A quality, high-power rifle scope should provide crisp, clear, edge-to-edge resolution without sacrificing eye relief.

A **fixed-power** rifle scope is recommended if a hunter finds himself shooting at the same distance without much variation. A fixed magnification allows a hands-free approach to shooting and is extremely rugged. In other words, the hunter does not have to readjust power settings in order to get the shot. A premium quality 4- or 6-power rifle scope is sufficient for conditions up to 500 yards, though 6-power will create problems in focusing on relatively close targets.

The hunter who shoots under diverse conditions needs a **variable-power** rifle scope, which allows adjustment from low to high magnification. Variables provide a wide field of view for close-range shooting or brushy terrain when set at low power. Higher magnifications provide greater detail on the target and longer shots in open areas. A variable scope from 3 to 9X, with a 42mm objective, is a perfect combination because the power and field of view can be adapted to any hunting situation.

Rifle scopes contain a number of highly polished lenses. One-half of the light that enters the objective lens can be lost or reflected before it reaches the eye, resulting in decreased accuracy. To counter this, lenses are treated with a thin, anti-reflective (AR) coating formulated to allow 90 percent of light transmission to reach the eye. A single reflective coating on all glass surfaces may still allow 18 to 22 percent of the light to be lost. Multicoated scopes may only allow 11 to 15 percent to be lost.

Bullets: Ballistic Coefficient & Sectional Density

Ballistic Coefficient is a measure of how aerodynamic a bullet is and how well it cuts through the air. The higher the number, the less the bullet is slowed by air resistance over a given distance at a given velocity. That means a higher BC bullet retains its velocity better than a low BC bullet, resulting in flatter trajectories and increased down-range energy retention.

A pointed bullet will have a higher BC than a flat-nosed or round-nosed bullet of the same diameter and weight simply because it offers less wind resistance.

Sectional Density is a measure of a bullet's mass relative to its cross-section: in simple terms, a relationship of its weight to its diameter.

The higher the SD of a bullet in a given diameter, the heavier and longer that bullet will be. From a big game hunter's standpoint the most relevant measure of SD is that with all else being equal, the higher the SD of a bullet the better its ability to penetrate.

—Bryce Towsley

WHITE-TAILED DEER

HUNTER:
Stuart Hagen

RESIDENCE:
Mondovi, WI

WHERE TAKEN:
Buffalo County, Wisconsin

ARMS USED:
Winchester Model 70 .30-06 Rifle

Stuart's 10-pointer fell on the last day of the season!

HUNTER:
Richard M. Ertel

RESIDENCE:
Spotsylvania, VA

WHERE TAKEN:
Culpeper County, Virginia

ARMS USED:
Knight .50 Caliber Disc.
Muzzleloader

Shotgun Cleaning Tips

C leaning a shotgun after a day of shooting is like washing dishes after eating a great meal. It's not the part you look forward to. Immediate gun cleaning, however, is just as necessary as kitchen chores.

As a shotgun tube cools, condensation occurs. Plastic wad and powder fouling attracts moisture and hardens, trapping that moisture against the walls of the tube. Rust and even pitting can occur.

Venco Industries offers these cleaning tips:

• Use only phosphorous bronze brushes that are wound on a core; they are much more durable and flexible.

• Commercial gun cleaning kits are fine, but there are home products you can use as substitutes. For example, an excellent patch rod can be made from a $5/8$-inch wooden dowel with a bicycle handlebar grip fastened to one end.

• An absorbent paper towel folded and rolled to bore-filling diameter is an excellent cleaning patch. Soak the towel with a quality bore cleaner and push it the length of the bore from chamber to muzzle. Wet the brush and patch until they come out clean.

• Use a toothbrush to scrub bearing surfaces with a commercial cleaner/lubricant. Then wipe it off and coat the metal surfaces, including the inside of the tube, with a quality moisture displacer/rust preventative.

Elk

CERVUS ELAPHUS

OTHER NAMES:
Wapiti, Yellowstone elk, Rocky
Mountain elk

CHARACTERISTICS:
Coat brown (pale yellowish in old
bulls); head, neck and legs darker than
rest of body; distinctive rump patch
yellowish to almost orange; mane or ruff
longer on bulls than on cows; antlers of
mature bulls generally have five tines
projecting from the main branch for a
total of six points; bulls can weigh more
than 1,000 pounds before the rut but
seldom exceed 900 pounds during
hunting season; cows weigh 500 to 600
pounds.

HABITAT:
Mainly coniferous forests interspersed
with natural or man-made openings
(mountain meadows, grasslands, burns
and logged areas).

FOOD:
Grasses, sedges, forbs, sagebrush, decid-
uous shrubs (especially willow and serviceberry) and young trees (especially
chokecherry and aspen), some conifers.

BEHAVIOR:
Strong herding instinct; old cows usually
lead summer herds of cows, calves and
yearling (spike) bulls; in many parts of
their range, elk summer at higher eleva-
tions and move down to grass and/or
shrub winter ranges (with nearby trees
for thermal cover) or to established
feedgrounds; habitat use strongly influ-
enced by human activities.

REPRODUCTION:
Breed in September and early October;
one spotted calf; shed antlers during
March or April; bulls gather and hold
harems, challenge one another by
bugling; cows usually breed when $2^1/2$
years old.

HUNTING:
The best time to hunt elk is during
the rut, when calling can bring in
an angry bull looking to defend
his harem. These days, if you
hunt the rut, you'll probably
have to do it with a bow or
maybe a muzzleloader.

TIPS AFIELD

Small Game Field Care

You've shot a rabbit, a hare or a squirrel. Now what? If you want to have it mounted, carefully wipe off any blood or dirt from its fur, plug the nostrils, mouth and any shot holes with cotton or pieces of dry cloth. Place the animal neatly in a heavy plastic bag and freeze it solid before taking it to the taxidermist.

More likely, you are going to want to eat your small game. Here's how to handle it afield, according to the National Rifle Association:

- Open the body cavity from the neck to the anal vent to remove all entrails, after freeing them from all connective tissue. Exercise care in cutting around anal/genital area to avoid meat contamination.

- Cut the animal into serving size pieces—four legs and thighs and the body.

- To skin the animal, work your fingers between the skin and body until they meet at the back. Then grasp the skin in one hand, the body in the other. The skin will now break with a sharp tug. Tougher skin on a squirrel should be cut.

- Skin can now be peeled off freely in both directions and cut off, along with the head, feet and tail.

Come Hell, High Water or Thin Ice

BY NAHC MEMBER DANIEL JAMES HENDRICKS

One cold November day I was headed southwest from my hometown of Glenwood, Minnesota. The ground was snow covered, and there was a raw west wind to remind me that winter had settled in for a long, irritating stay.

The fact that pheasant season was still open kept me alert. I had my double barrel along just in case.

As I headed down the state highway, I happened to glance down one of the gravel township roads and saw a large rooster saunter out of the knee-high grass. I checked my plat map of the area to confirm that I had permission to hunt this property. I did.

As my car approached, the pheasant took to the air and flew into the swamp. I watched its flight and marked the area where the bird landed at the edge of a frozen pond.

I parked, uncased and loaded my gun, and headed toward my quarry.

The thunder of wings was all it took for me instinctively to move the butt of my shotgun to my shoulder. As the bird's silhouette rose above the cattails, I swung to my mark and fired the first shot: a clean miss.

I slowed on the second shot and made a clean hit. The bird folded up and crashed to the ice 50 feet out from the edge of the slough.

When I walked to the edge of the pond, both of my feet broke through the ice, and I sank up to my knees in cold water.

I pushed my foot into the boot, twisted it to lock it in and tried to free it. With a loud sucking noise, first one foot was freed and then the other.

I stepped back into the cattails to ponder and determine the value of the bird on the frozen pond. The only thought I had was, "I killed it; I am going to eat it." Now, it was a matter of how I was going to get at it.

Struck by a wonderful idea, I trudged back through the undergrowth to my car and headed home. I rummaged through my garage to gather the equipment to complete my mission: my fishing pole and tackle box, which contained a number of Dardevle spoons.

Back at the edge of the pond, I cast my lure over frozen water to snag the pheasant. Only in Minnesota could one get such diversity—one minute you're hunting pheasant, the next minute you're fishing for the same species.

What I had thought was a great idea was not easy. After dozens of casts with no results, I began to forget about the taste of roast pheasant, and I became more aware of what the wind was doing to my bare hands. Just when I was getting really concerned about frostbite, I snagged the bird. I began to drag it toward me. It came about 2 feet, then stopped. One of the treble hooks of the Dardevle had snagged the ice.

Placing the tip of my rod high in the air, I began a series of sharp tugs. Something gave, but it wasn't the Dardevle. My line snapped.

Fifteen feet out on the ice I could see the end of the line that had betrayed me. I already had too much invested in this little adventure, so I did what I knew I must. I dropped to a spread-eagle position and crawled out on the ice. I hoped that by distributing my weight I might trick the ice into allowing me to pass.

The theory must have been sound, because I reached the end of the line, grabbed it with my teeth and returned to shore without causing the ice to crack.

Once I was back on the edge of the pond, I stood and began to gently tug on the end of the line. To my dismay I felt it give again. This time the line broke at the lure.

When the line snapped, the end came flying in my direction, leaving the pheasant and the Dardevle. Stunned, I considered my latest setback. Then I reasoned that if the ice had held me 15 feet out, why not 50?

Back on my hands and knees, I was once more on my belly. As I covered the distance, I became more adept at my new method of movement. The farther I went, the more intense the danger became and the faster I moved.

By the time I reached the bird, my heart was pounding and the sweat was pouring out of my pores, cold or no cold. I grabbed the pheasant, put it in my mouth and took off for shore. Sliding and crawling across the ice, I hit high gear about 40 feet from the pond's edge. I made the trip back much faster than going out.

The elation I felt when I got my feet back on hard ground was one I won't soon forget. I salvaged my supper. On the way to the car, I spit out feathers and evaluated the pros and cons of owning a good hunting dog.

I must add that I never enjoyed the taste of pheasant as much as I did when I ate that particular bird!

How to Get Rattlin' Antlers Without Gettin' Your Hands Dirty

BY DON DINNDORF

ALL IN FUN

Hunters who rattle for deer get their antlers one of two ways: They either buy them or bag a buck and use the deer's antlers.

'Course, there are exceptions.

Like Ken Hiemenz, from St. Joseph, Minnesota.

Hiemenz got himself a real pair of rattlin' antlers from a live whitetail without taking his knife from its sheath. He did fire a shot—but didn't get his hands dirty.

As far as I know, what Hiemenz did had never been done before. And it's safe to say it won't happen again for some time.

Before sunrise on opening day of the Minnesota firearm deer season, Hiemenz climbed into his treestand. He overlooked a woodlot near St. Joe, and hoped to spy a buck as it returned from an evening meal in one of the adjoining fields.

It wasn't long before he did.

As the sun broke free of the horizon, Hiemenz saw a deer. The deer was walking on a trail that would bring it within gun range of the treestand.

Hiemenz waited patiently as the deer approached. Slowly bringing the bolt-action rifle to his shoulder, Hiemenz peered through the scope. The deer sported a small 8-point rack.

In his present position, Hiemenz was a bit off balance. While he looked at the rack through his scope, he shifted his weight to his right foot.

"Kaboom!"

His rifle discharged as he shifted his weight. Hiemenz looked at the gun in disbelief, then bolted another .308 Win. cartridge and took a shot at the buck as it escaped into thick cover.

Shaking his head at what had happened, Hiemenz watched and listened for sign that the buck was hit. But

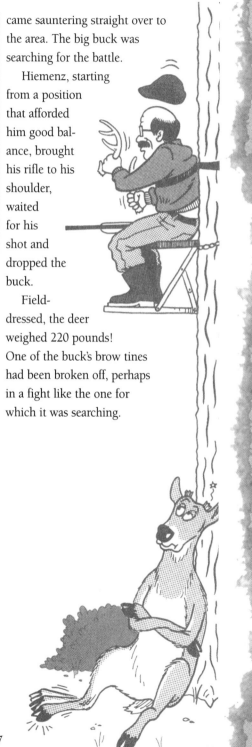

the deer didn't go down. It just kept going.

Hiemenz mentally marked the location where he had spotted the deer, the place where he saw it enter the thick cover and the direction he last heard the deer moving.

He climbed down from his treestand and walked to the spot where the deer had been standing. He started to check for blood or any sign that he had hit the deer. To his surprise, he found a 4-point antler on the ground. The antler appeared to have been shot off just below the brow tine. Four feet away lay the other antler, this one clipped off just above the juncture of the antler with the skull.

Hiemenz was joined by his son. Together they scoured the area for any sign that the bullet had hit anything besides both antlers. Despite their efforts, they didn't locate any blood or sign that the deer was injured. Apparently, the 8-point whitetail had run off unhurt.

In the early afternoon of that same day, Hiemenz returned to his stand and placed it higher in the tree.

Sitting there studying his new antlers, Hiemenz realized that he might be able to put them to good use. He began rattling vigorously, slamming and shaking the antlers together to simulate the sounds of deer fighting. For 2 hours there was no response. But Hiemenz kept at it.

Then a big-bodied 7-point whitetail came sauntering straight over to the area. The big buck was searching for the battle.

Hiemenz, starting from a position that afforded him good balance, brought his rifle to his shoulder, waited for his shot and dropped the buck.

Field-dressed, the deer weighed 220 pounds! One of the buck's brow tines had been broken off, perhaps in a fight like the one for which it was searching.

SOMETHING TO SHOOT FOR

WHITE-TAILED DEER

HUNTER:
Steve Otrupcak

RESIDENCE:
Little Falls, NY

WHERE TAKEN:
Little Falls, New York

ARMS USED:
Browning Auto 12 Gauge Shotgun

Steve's 12-pointer, taken close to home, was actually a 5x7. It weighed 191 pounds.

HUNTER:
Nick Arena

RESIDENCE:
Lynbrook, NY

WHERE TAKEN:
Canada

ARMS USED:
Browning 7mm Mag A Bolt
Rifle

Get Your Gun Ready

GETTING READY

I t makes sense to check your gun before you are actually ready to use it afield. A few precautions can mean the difference between ecstacy and disappointment. Besides sighting it in, to make sure it is shooting accurately, here are some things you should do:

- If the bore is clean and has been stored for awhile, run a clean cloth through the barrel to wipe away any oil.

- Work the action repeatedly and, if possible, cycle a few dummy rounds through the gun.

- Look the gun over thoroughly. Any shiny surfaces on moving parts can signal wear. A touch of grease on the shiny parts keeps things running smoothly. A rule of thumb is that if you can see the grease after it's been applied, you've used too much.

- Dry fire your rifle or shotgun to reacquaint yourself with just where the trigger "breaks." In old guns, use snap caps to protect the firing pin.

- Check and tighten, if necessary, screws in guards, scope mounts and other sights. Use a screwdriver ground to fit the screws. Few things mar the appearance of a good gun more than screws chewed up by poorly fitting screwdrivers.

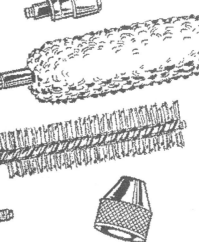

A Turkey Hunter's Code of Conduct

The National Wild Turkey Federation has been a prime mover in the conservation of the wild turkey and the preservation of turkey hunting. Among its contributions is this code of conduct that it has enumerated. As a responsible turkey hunter, I will:

1 Not let peer pressure or the excitement of the hunt cloud my judgment.

2 Learn and practice safe hunting techniques.

3 Hunt the wild turkey fairly.

4 Know the capabilities and limitations of my gun or bow and use it safely.

5 Obey and support all wildlife laws and report all variations.

6 Respect the land and the landowner and always obtain permission before hunting.

7 Avoid knowingly interfering with another hunter and respect the right of others to lawfully share the outdoors.

8 Value the hunting experience and appreciate the beauty of the wild turkey.

9 Positively identify my target as a legal bird and insist on a good shot.

10 Share responsible turkey hunting with others and work for wild turkey conservation.

WILD TURKEY

NAME:
John K. Becvar Sr. and
James P. Becvar

RESIDENCE:
Johnston, IA

WHERE TAKEN:
Johnston, Iowa

ARMS USED:
Remington 1100 Shotgun;
$2^3/4$-Inch No. 4 Winchester
Mags

Dad and son show off the Becvar spring turkey harvest: $25^1/2$-and $23^1/2$-pound toms. The heavier bird sported a 10-inch beard, the "lighter" one a 9-inch beard.

NAME:
Joseph Pizzonia

RESIDENCE:
Hollis, NY

WHERE TAKEN:
Shohola, Pennsylvania

ARMS USED:
Mossberg Shotgun;
$3^1/2$-inch No. 6 Shot

NAHC member Joseph Pizzonia, far right, enjoyed a very successful spring outing with three buddies. Joe's gobbler weighed 20 pounds and wore a 10-inch beard.

HUNTING HUMOR

Tomasic art

"You'll have to admit—even for
a mountain goat, he's good."

Easy Field Care for Birds

You've downed a prized game bird. Decide what you want to do with it.

If you want to mount it, the National Rifle Association suggests you carefully wipe off any blood or dirt from its feathers, plug its nostrils, beak and any holes with tissue, cotton or cloth, then freeze it in a heavy plastic bag before taking it to the taxidermist.

If you simply wish to prepare it for the table, then hold the belly up in one hand and draw out the entrails through a single cut from breastbone to vent. Then pluck the feathers or remove the entire skin, along with its wings, head, feet and tail. To make the plucking easier, scald the bird. For waterfowl, dip them in hot wax or paraffin to ease feather removal.

Did You know?

Studies indicate that white-tailed deer make 12 different sounds. Understanding these calls could help you bag a trophy. According to James Schrenkel, wildlife biologist with Alabama Game, Fish & Wildlife, these 12 sounds can be divided into 5 categories:

1 **Alarm and distress calls.** The snort is the most recognized by hunters.

2 **Antagonistic or aggressive calls.** These are a series of grunts and snorts. Antagonistic calls express dominance or aggression. Both bucks and does use these calls.

3 **Mating calls.** The most common is a tending grunt.

4 **Maternal-neonatal calls.** The most common is the bleat. Fawns are the only deer that make this call. A bleating fawn is simply seeking attention from its doe. The doe's maternal call is not a bleat, but a grunt-like sound used to locate or call the fawn.

5 **Contact calls.** Made only by does, these allow a group of deer to keep in contact with one another even when visual contact is lost.

TIPS AFIELD

Basic Tactics for Bagging More Bunnies
BY GREGG GUTSCHOW

If you don't have a hound, hunt slowly. Rustle every possible rabbit cover. Pause and scan openings. If you spot a statue-still rabbit, be ready to shoot; your first move might send him running.

Calm, sunny winter days with temperatures above freezing often lure rabbits from their holes to soak up the sun and grab a snack. Snow also makes sign and rabbits themselves more visible. Study sign to figure out their preferred habitats.

Generally, rabbits are most active in the morning and late in the afternoon.

In the North, however, cottontails often venture out during the warmest midday hours.

A shotgun, from .410 to 12 gauge is okay, provided it is choked no more tightly than modified. Improved cylinder is probably the best all-around cottontail choke. You don't need much punch to be effective; lightly loaded economical shells with No. 6 lead and packaged under the "Game Load" specification are usually enough.

Wear a hunter-orange cap and vest to give you visibility in the thick cover rabbit hunting often takes you.

WATERFOWL

NAME:
John Michael Allen

RESIDENCE:
Boulder City, NV

WHERE TAKEN:
California

ARMS USED:
Mossberg 500 Shotgun

John got these mallards with some sharp shooting, fortified by No. 2 steel shot.

NAME:
Lloyd Dykstra

RESIDENCE:
Junction City, OR

WHERE TAKEN:
Near Junction City, Oregon

ARMS USED:
Browning 10GT 12 Gauge Shotgun

Lloyd, right, with his hunting buddy, Mark Harrington, and the impressive line-up of ducks they took close to home.

Retaining Access to Hunting Lands

NOTICE

NO TRESPASSING ON THIS PROPERTY UNDER PENALTY OF THE LAW

If you hunt on private property that is not yours, you know how grateful you should be for the right to access that land. Don't ever take that access for granted. Here are ways to help ensure that you will retain permission to hunt—suggestions from the National Rifle Association:

1 Respect the landowner's property as you would your own.

2 Don't litter. Carry away any litter left by others.

3 Leave gates as you find them. Cross fences in a manner that will not break or loosen wires or posts.

4 Don't shoot toward homes, buildings, livestock, pets or high-wire lines.

5 Hunt only those areas designated by the landowner.

6 Don't walk through unharvested crops or garden areas.

7 Don't hunt near areas containing livestock or pets.

8 Keep your dog under control, especially when near domestic animals or livestock.

9 Park your car only where the landowner has designated.

10 Offer to share some of your game with the landowner.

11 Hunt in small groups when appropriate.

12 Thank the landowner at the conclusion of the day's hunt.

MULE DEER

HUNTER:
Joseph M. Hanson

RESIDENCE:
Las Vegas, NV

WHERE TAKEN:
Crestone, Colorado

ARMS USED:
.300 Weatherby Mag Rifle

A Hunter's Pledge

 esponsible hunting provides unique challenges and rewards. However, the future of the sport depends on each hunter's behavior and ethics. Therefore, as a hunter, I pledge to:

- Respect the environment and wildlife.
- Respect property and landowners.
- Show consideration for nonhunters.
- Hunt safely.
- Know and obey the law.
- Support wildlife and habitat conservation.
- Pass on an ethical hunting tradition.
- Strive to improve my outdoors skills and understanding of wildlife.
- Hunt only with ethical hunters.

By following these principles of conduct each time I go afield, I will give my best to the sport, the public, the environment and myself. The responsibility to hunt ethically is mine; the future of hunting depends on me.

DEER HUNTER'S CHECKLIST

There's nothing worse than getting to hunting camp only to discover that you've forgotten something you really need to have. The Pennsylvania Game Commission offers this checklist. The commission calls it "The Complete Deer Hunter's Checklist," but we're not really sure that such a checklist could ever be complete. In fact, we've added a few items and left space for you to add some more! Make copies of this, and add listings that apply to your needs. This could apply to more than just deer hunting, but you might have to add items such as "decoys" or other items for specialty hunting.

The commission suggests that you put a slash (/) through a box to the left of the item when it is secured; then put a back slash (\) through the box to make an X when the item is actually packed.

PRESEASON CHECKPOINTS
- ❑ Purchase hunting licenses
- ❑ Study hunting regulations
- ❑ Know tagging system
- ❑ Secure landowner's permission
- ❑ Complete hunter safety course
- ❑ Preseason scouting
- ❑ Physical fitness program
- ❑ Sighting-in and practice

- ❑ Equipment cleaning and repair
- ❑ Schedule vacation time
- ❑ Make camp repairs
- ❑ Vehicle maintenance

PRESEASON NOTES: _____

_____

_____

_____

CLOTHING

- ❑ Check weather report and make appropriate selections
- ❑ Hat (required amount of hunter orange)
- ❑ Coat
- ❑ Jacket
- ❑ Vest
- ❑ Coveralls
- ❑ Pants
- ❑ Shirts
- ❑ Sweater
- ❑ Boots (with liners and insoles; check laces)
- ❑ Hipboots
- ❑ Regular and liner socks
- ❑ Gloves or mittens
- ❑ Thermal underwear
- ❑ Belt, suspenders
- ❑ Handkerchief, bandanna
- ❑ Raingear
- ❑ Scarf
- ❑ Gaiters
- ❑ Face mask

CLOTHING NOTES: _____

_____

_____

_____

OPTICS

- ❑ Scope (check rings and mounts for tightness)
- ❑ Scope cover/lens cap
- ❑ Binoculars
- ❑ Shooting glasses
- ❑ Sunglasses
- ❑ Lens cleaning tissues
- ❑ Anti-fog spray
- ❑ Regular eyeglasses
- ❑ Spotting scope
- ❑ Rangefinder
- ❑ Camera, film and accessories
- ❑ Camcorder

OPTICS NOTES: _____

_____

_____

_____

Continued ...

Guns, Ammo & Related Items

- ❑ Gunsmithing
- ❑ Handloading
- ❑ Rifle (sighted-in, cleaned)
- ❑ Handgun (sighted-in, cleaned)
- ❑ Shotgun (sighted-in, cleaned)
- ❑ Sling or carrying strap
- ❑ Spare clip
- ❑ Gun case
- ❑ Ammunition (correct caliber or gauge; same load with which firearm was sighted-in)
- ❑ Cartridge carrier
- ❑ Gun cleaning kit for field or camp

GUN NOTES: _____

_____

_____

Personal Items/Other Checkpoints

- ❑ Prescription medicine
- ❑ Wallet with I.D., money, credit cards
- ❑ Keys to camp, gun case, extra vehicle keys
- ❑ Vehicle safety and fluids check
- ❑ Check for varying weather conditions
- ❑ Fuel up
- ❑ Set alarm clock (put in new batteries)
- ❑ Leave detailed hunting itinerary for family
- ❑ Cellular phone

PERSONAL ITEM NOTES: _____

_____

_____

_____

AFTER THE HUNT & POST SEASON

- ❑ Mail in harvest report card
- ❑ Process deer
- ❑ Taxidermy arrangements
- ❑ Clean and store all gear
- ❑ Return borrowed gear
- ❑ Get film processed
- ❑ Send landowner thank you note
- ❑ Share the harvest

POST-SEASON NOTES: _____

_____

_____

FIELD GEAR & ACCESSORIES

- ❑ Knife, sharpened
- ❑ Bone saw
- ❑ Pruning shares
- ❑ Flashlight (new bulb, new batteries, spare bulb, spare batteries)
- ❑ Drag rope
- ❑ License, license holder
- ❑ Pen and string or wire for tagging
- ❑ Deer sled or cart
- ❑ Field-dressing kit (wet towlettes, rubber gloves, plastic bag)
- ❑ Compass
- ❑ Topo maps
- ❑ GPS
- ❑ Masking scents
- ❑ Deer calls
- ❑ Water bottle, canteen or bota, filled with water
- ❑ Thermos
- ❑ Survival kit
- ❑ First-aid kit
- ❑ Whistle
- ❑ Hunting seat
- ❑ Hunter's seat cushion
- ❑ Treestand (with safety belt and accessories)
- ❑ Plastic urinal
- ❑ Pocket hand warmers
- ❑ Toilet tissue
- ❑ Daypack/fanny pack, duffle bag
- ❑ Lunch/field snacks
- ❑ Watch
- ❑ High-visibility surveyor tape
- ❑ Insect repellant

FIELD GEAR NOTES: _____

_____

_____

Recipes

One-Pan Venison

Ingredients

Parsley

Garlic

Bacon (2 strips per steak)

Salt and Pepper

Seasoned Flour

Chicken Broth (2 cups)

Cotton Twine

Preparation

Tenderize steaks with mallet, remove any bones, season with parsley and garlic
to taste. In semi-deep pan, brown bacon. Place bacon in middle of steak, then
roll steaks and tie with cotton twine. Roll steaks in flour seasoned with salt and
pepper. Place steaks in same pan that bacon was cooked and brown steaks in
bacon grease. After browning, drain off excess fat, then pour chicken broth
over steaks. Let simmer until steaks are cooked through, usually 30 to 40 minutes. Broth and flour make their own gravy. Total prep and cook time: 45 to 60
minutes.

Greg Kollar
Lawton, OK

Bighorn Sheep

OVIS CANADENSIS

OTHER NAMES:

Rocky Mountain sheep, Rocky Mountain bighorn, bighorn

CHARACTERISTICS:

Coat grayish-brown with yellowish-white underparts; creamy-white rump patch around small brown tail; horns of adult rams massive and curled, up to 45 inches long; horns of adult ewes thin, slightly curved, 6 to 13 inches long; horns of yearling rams wider at the base with more divergent tips than those of ewes and 7.5 to 17 inches long; old rams may exceed 300 pounds, ewes seldom exceed 150 pounds.

HABITAT:

Cliffs, mountain slopes, rolling foothills; sometimes cross intermountain valleys.

FOOD:

Bunchgrasses and shrubs on winter range; wide variety of grasses, sedges and forbs on summer range.

BEHAVIOR:

A very sociable big game species; herds segregate according to age and sex; ewes, lambs and yearling males band together; adult males band in herds spanning 2- or 3-year classes; subject to die-offs

related to severe winter weather and pneumonia.

REPRODUCTION:

Breed in November; usually one young; rams battle for dominance by crashing horns together; ewes usually breed at $2^1/_2$ years of age, but may breed as yearlings.

HUNTING:

Bighorns have been reintroduced into many historic ranges and you can get a tag if you save your pennies and have some luck. Sheep are tough to hunt because you have to work to get into good sheep country, way "out back." Once there, glass hard and shoot well and you'll bring home some horns.

ALL IN FUN

THE GREAT GROUSE GOD

BY DON FEIGERT

Other hunters try to tell me ruffed grouse are stupid, second-rate birds, not as crafty as crows or as elusive as woodcocks. All I can figure is they must be referring to grouse in other states, where they've never been hunted, because the birds I hunt are smarter than brain surgeons and trickier than your Congressman.

Pennsylvania grouse are free spirit types who laugh at the poor fools pushing through briars and brambles, crawling and falling over thick-limbed blow-downs just to glimpse these lively gamebirds as they disappear into safety among the hemlocks and the aspens. The grouse I hunt either flush at 50 yards or hold tight in those thickets so binding a hunter can't get his gun up, let alone swing, aim and pull the trigger.

You can't tell me these birds aren't smart. They're smarter than your ex-wife's divorce lawyer. Or else they're the luckiest creatures alive. Or else they have mindless instincts or built-in collision-avoidance radar that prevents them from ever occupying the same place and time as size $7^1/_2$ shot pellets. Or else there is a guardian god of grouse in Pennsylvania who guides them through their daily lives. What a powerful and

persistent being that god must be. I believe the red gods of hunting hide when the grouse god enters the woods.

Last fall, for example, I was hunting mountaintop thickets along an old, abandoned logging road, when I actually spotted a ruffed grouse sitting tight in front of me under the branches of a windfall. I could see the little turkey tail and the dark feathers of the back. I stared in wonder for a moment, then looked up and surveyed the cover.

"My goodness, what a careless grouse," I thought. "With no element of surprise in its favor, no unexpected shock of thundering wings, how can this bird escape the deadly pattern of my reliable Remington?"

With a smile of confidence, I stepped forward and flushed the bird.

The grouse took off from my left in a straightaway flight, the easiest possible shot, and I turned to take him. But as the gun barrel swung sideways, it smacked hard against a 2-inch-diameter sapling and sent me reverberating off-balance in the other direction. I swear that tree had not been there a moment earlier. It was grown in the way at the critical time by the guardian of the grouse.

I remember a day when I wrestled through thick laurel, grapevines and oak all morning, flushing an even dozen ruffed grouse and not firing a shot. Every time a bird took off, I was bending under branches or elbowing through thickets, and each time I was out of position to swing and shoot.

Finally, I rousted a colorful bird at the edge of a clearing and watched it dart wide open in a twisting flight. Each time my gun zigged, however, the grouse zagged, and I missed 3 shots. I stood there then, clutching my emptied shotgun, as the grouse god signaled "all clear," and 6 more thunder chickens took off across the clearing one at a time. I swear the last one chuckled as it fluttered slowly overhead, well within range of my spent shotgun.

Someone or something is protecting these birds, no doubt about it. If I didn't have a sense of humor, these grouse and their guardian god would drive me crazy.

Maybe grouse hunting would be easier and more productive if I tried the "drive and block" method with other hunters or used modern technology. If a hunter walked the woodlands playing a tape recording of people falling down over blowdown logs and cursing, for example, he would surely see many rubberneck grouse fluttering above to laugh and stare. I know from experience that these birds love to taunt human beings lying on the ground. I've looked up and caught their smirks.

We Pennsylvania hunters are generally too proud and stubborn for teamwork or trickery, though. We hunt remote coverts far from dirt access roads, where only the wildest and spookiest of ruffed grouse abide. And where the grouse god travels in majesty. I walk miles of rugged forest every hunting day to search out these coverts of joyful feathered frustration. I do this gladly and with irrational hope for success.

I would not recommend Pennsylvania grouse hunting to any of you tenderfoot hunters from the tame-grouse states. Only veterans like myself of 1,000 shotgun misses can appreciate the special breed of ruffed grouse that thrive and die of old age or laughter in the wild grouse state. So don't come to Pennsylvania to hunt grouse. Stay home and enjoy your own stupid, suicidal birds. Ours are too smart for you.

TIPS AFIELD

Stay on Track

Sport utility (SUV) and all terrain vehicles (ATV) are providing growing numbers of hunters with greater access to hunting areas, but there is also concern about the damage that these vehicles potentially pose to wildlife habitat, especially on public lands.

"Use of vehicles off established roads and trails can damage habitat by causing erosion and by destroying vegetation that provides food and cover for wildlife. It also reflects poorly on hunters and can be used as a weapon by those who oppose recreational hunting," says Mike Cox of the Nevada Division of Wildlife.

Cox knows that SUVs and ATVs offer real advantages in hauling people, equipment and downed game over rough roads, but he cautions that driving the vehicles off established roads to pursue game is unethical.

Wildlife managers note that vehicle tire tracks blazed by an inconsiderate off-road driver are an invitation for other vehicles to follow that same route. The cumulative effect results in habitat being lost as a trail is created. It may also result in a hunter giving away a favorite hunting location to others.

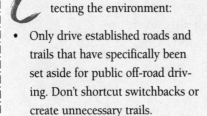

"Do Not Disturb"

Chevy Truck urges every off-roader to follow these basic rules for protecting the environment:

- Only drive established roads and trails that have specifically been set aside for public off-road driving. Don't shortcut switchbacks or create unnecessary trails.

- Avoid any driving practice that could damage the environment or disturb wildlife (e.g., wheel-spinning, running over young trees and shrubs, or unnecessarily driving through streams or soft ground.

- Leave nature the way you found it. Remove all refuse from the campsite before leaving.

- Take extreme caution with open fires, camp stoves and lanterns.

- When possible, avoid wet roads and trails, wetlands and meadows. Remember a degraded trail today is a *closed* one tomorrow.

SOMETHING TO SHOOT FOR

MULE DEER

HUNTER:
Larry Bell

RESIDENCE:
Fallon, NV

WHERE TAKEN:
Nevada

ARMS USED:
.25-06 Rifle; Hand Loads

HUNTER:
Dwayne Prins

RESIDENCE:
Canon City, CO

WHERE TAKEN:
Gunnison, Colorado

ARMS USED:
.300 Weatherby Mag Rifle

Alfred's Lucky Charm

BY JEFF BOEHLER

"Trow one der, ya, right der, Cheff," another decoy splashed into the darkness and out of sight as it left my flashlight's beam. "Good ... good spot, Cheff," Alfred praised. Alfred McKay, our French Canadian guide, and I took our time setting out the hodgepodge spread of well-used decoys. Alfred had driven my father-in-law Mert and me out to the cattail point two hours before sunrise to lay claim to it for the day. "Dis is agood spread of decoys, Cheff, but we're missing my lucky charm." I just nodded and Alfred didn't need a lot of prodding. "Der's one leetle bluebill dat is da cutest decoy I ever seen. Whenever I hunt wit it, we get lots of dem ducks. I was planning to take it home for my mantle, but someone done walked off wit it before I could take it for myself."

The oars squeaked as Alfred guided our homemade wooden skiff back to shore. It was still pitch dark and I was anxious for the sunrise, to see for myself this famous Delta Marsh I'd heard so much about. Jimmy Robinson made the Delta Marsh famous with all the stories he wrote about its ducks, guides and hunters. It was fitting that I was here at the Crooked Creek Lodge with a group from the Minneapolis Fur, Fin and Feather Club, a club that Jimmy Robinson started in 1940.

"Der's one, Cheff," Alfred warned. I swung my Benelli in front of the mallard, pulled the trigger and watched as my first official Delta Marsh duck splashed into the water among the decoys. Minutes later, a bull canvasback caught us off guard and Mert was lucky to get off a hurried shot.

"Cheff ... Cheff, you got to pull da treeger if you're goin ta get dem ducks," the ribbing from Alfred was starting, and he was only getting warmed up. "Are you a conservationist, Cheff? Ya, you must be a conservationist, letting dat pretty can fly by." Our first morning actually turned out to be slow hunting. It was too warm, with too little wind. But no matter. What we lacked in ducks, we made up for in laughter. Alfred kept us entertained with his good natured teasing as well as stories of his adventures on the famed marsh.

From his tales, it was easy to see that fun seems to follow him wherever he goes. The features on his weather tanned face are slightly exaggerated, like a character in a Norman Rockwell painting. When he smiles his whole face lights up like a Christmas tree and his eyes sparkle like a boy looking for mischief.

By lunchtime Alfred had deemed my father-in-law and me "Pork and Bean." You know you're with the right group when at 6' 2" and 200 pounds you're called the skinny guy and forced to squeeze into the chair by the window at mealtime.

That afternoon, Alfred took us to a more remote spot on the vast marsh by means of an Argo. This wonderful machine is a cross between an ATV and a tank, and it carried us into a location otherwise inaccessible. When we arrived, there was a boat and decoys waiting. "Cheff, here's my lucky charm!" Alfred beamed as he lifted a cute little bluebill decoy from the bottom of the boat and tossed it to the outer edge of the decoys. He was right. It was brighter and much prettier than any of the other decoys we'd used. "Someone didn't take her, dat's good ... dat's good." Alfred was delighted.

His lucky charm worked. We were swarmed by ducks that afternoon: cans, redheads, mallards, teal—a virtual smorgasbord of Delta ducks. We had a great duck shoot, the type you'd like to play over and over again to shoot at the ones you let fly by and hit the ones you missed.

The next day we were with different guides, lying among the wheat stubble and Canada goose shells. We had a heck

Continued ...

79

of a goose shoot as they came off the refuge. After lunch back at the lodge, we piled into the owner's truck for an afternoon of sharptail hunting. "Cheff, you got to pull da treeger on dose grouse if you're gonna get dem birds," Alfred joked.

After breakfast on our last morning, I saw Alfred in the kitchen. "Cheff, I scout out my secret spot for Pork and Bean today. You guys will get dem ducks today, boy!" When he found out he had been paired with different hunters I could hear him with John, the owner, in the other room, "I got special spot for Mert and Cheff today, I tink I should take dem boys out." Alfred wasn't our guide that last day, but we all rode out to the marsh together.

After the morning's hunt we picked up Alfred and his hunters. As we loaded their gear into the trailer behind the Argo, Alfred pulled his lucky charm decoy from the boat and stashed it in the trailer. Obviously he was finally taking the bluebill home for a comfortable retirement on his fireplace mantle.

Mert and I took pictures with Alfred before we said goodbye. Alfred even got his own camera to have his picture taken with "Pork and Bean." We loaded our truck full of camo, guns and gear while the guides sorted and packed our ducks and geese into our coolers. We had hours to talk about our trip as we drove south through Manitoba, North Dakota and Minnesota. When we got home, I unloaded some of Mert's gear as he took the cooler downstairs to the freezer to unload the ducks. When he came back upstairs he was grinning and holding the cutest little bluebill decoy. It was Alfred's lucky charm. Alfred had hidden it among our ducks after writing on its side: to Mert and Jeff, from Alfred McKay.

It now sits in my den, bringing back great memories of our duck hunt on the great Delta Marsh with our new friend, Alfred ... and his lucky charm.

TIPS AFIELD

Use Turkey Decoys Safely

Turkey decoys are a key to many a hunter's success, but due to their realistic appearance, coupled with the calling a hunter uses with his decoys, a decoy can be mistaken for the real thing by another hunter. And that could put the hunter in a dangerous situation. Here's what the National Wild Turkey Federation recommends you do to avoid an accident:

- A decoy should never be visible while being transported. Never carry an uncovered decoy any distance.

- Whenever possible, set up by a tree that is wider than your shoulders and taller than your head.

- From your seated position, identify the clearest line of vision to your front. Establish a "sight line" that allows you 100 yards visibility. Then set your decoy(s) approximately 20 yards from your position on the line.

- Should you see another hunter, especially one close to your line of sight, call out to them in a loud, clear voice. His presence has already compromised your location and a soft call may only confuse him, rather than alert him to your presence.

- If you are calling over decoys, then elect to move to a new location, before moving from your setup, check carefully to ensure that neither gobbler, predator nor hunter is stalking your decoys.

TIPS AFIELD

Big Bore, Big Pattern?

Acommon misconception among shotgunners is that a large gauge throws a larger pattern. After all, it's easier to score in skeet or trap with a 12 gauge gun than with a 20, isn't it?

Venco Industries, manufacturers of gun cleaning and lubricating products, poses that question—and provides the answer.

"Yes, it's easier to break birds with the bigger gauge, but not because of the size of the pattern. The rate of shot spread is controlled by the choke, not by the gauge," explains Joe Ventimiglia. "The pattern is about the same size whether it's from a 12, 16, 20 or 28 gauge. You'll probably score higher with a big bore because there are more pellets in the shot string—not because of the difference in the size of the pattern."

Types of Ballistics

The three common types of ballistics often referred to by shooters can be a little confusing. But it's really very simple.

Internal Ballistics. This is what happens inside the gun. It refers to the powder burning, pressure, the bullet's path down the barrel, etc.

External Ballistics. This is what happens during the bullet's flight through the air. It deals with trajectory, velocity, energy, etc.

Terminal Ballistics. This is what happens after the bullet has hit the target. It's the study of things such as expansion, weight retention, penetration, etc.

—Bryce Towsley

Grizzly Bear

URSUS ARCTOS

OTHER NAMES:

Brown bear, grizzly, silvertip

CHARACTERISTICS:

Coat brownish (but sometimes blond to almost black) with silver-tipped guard hairs; noticeable hump between shoulders; face looks slightly "dished-in"; claws on front feet are long (up to 4 inches) and nearly white; tracks show claw marks farther ahead of toes than those of black bears; males weigh 300 to 400 pounds, occasionally up to 650 pounds; even more in Alaska; females average 200 to 300 pounds.

HABITAT:

Tundra; seacoasts; coniferous forest mixed with open areas; alpine meadows; avalanche chutes; originally found on prairies along streams in the west.

FOOD:

Grasses, roots, bulbs, berries, insects, carrion, fish, rodents, occasional ungulates (wild or domestic) and garbage (where available).

BEHAVIOR:

Most active during early morning and late evening; gather and share concentrated food sources; dig dens into steep slopes at high elevation where snow accumulates and where roots support roof; adults climb trees with difficulty due to long, nearly straight claws.

REPRODUCTION:

Breed in June and July; one to four young (two most common) born naked and blind, develop in den before emerging in spring. Young usually remain with female until age 2. Females first breed at 4 to 6 years of age and breed in alternate years or every third year thereafter.

STATUS:

Main Wyoming populations are in and near Yellowstone National Park; not compatible with dense human populations.

HUNTING:

Although some grizzlies exist in the Lower 48, you can only hunt them in Alaska. Glass and spot and stalk with the wind in your favor. Use a big rifle and shoot well.

Grizzly at 30 Below

BY NAHC MEMBER KIM SEBASTIEN

Opelousas, Alabama, seemed like long ago and far away as I landed in the Eskimo village of Koyuk, Alaska, in mid-April. It was clear and extremely cold. I unloaded my gear and looked out over the frozen bay. There was no sign of the expected spring thaw. Bob Hannon of Big River Outfitters met me on the runway. We loaded my gear onto his sled and headed for base camp.

Bob's welcome was less than optimistic. Temperatures had dropped to 30 degrees below. A hunter and his guide had broken through ice while crossing a river. And the grizzlies were still in their dens.

The only good news was that one trophy-size grizzly was out. A hunter from Iowa and his guide had followed the mega-tracks of that lone bear for 13 days but hadn't caught a glimpse. The bear preferred dense stands of spruce where deadfalls and deep snow made travel nearly impossible.

The next day I teamed up with my guide. By midafternoon I was thankful I had spent 4 months getting in shape for the hunt. More than 100 miles from Koyuk in a small stand of spruce and willow, we dug out a hollow in the snow and ice to make camp. We never reached solid ground but laid spruce boughs on top of the ice for bedding.

Everything was frozen. For drinking water we chiseled ice from a nearby river and melted it on the Coleman stove. We drank the water warm; it froze if we let it sit.

My guide had experience hunting in Alaska's Brooks Range but never in this region. He was young and concerned about this new endeavor especially traveling across the snow and ice under limited visibility.

For a week we hunted in every direction, putting in long hours and experiencing bitter cold and often white-out conditions.

We covered many miles without seeing one track. My spirits were low; my confidence dwindled. We hoped for a break in the weather.

I had booked a 14-day hunt with Bob. But unbeknownst to my boss back home, I had made arrangements to hunt longer if necessary. I couldn't afford to come back here.

It was music to my ears the next morning when a snow machine drove up to our camp. It was an Eskimo from Koyuk, and he brought good news. We were going back to restock supplies, heal our bruises, warm our buns and hunt another area.

When I returned to base camp I met the Iowa hunter. He looked frazzled. He had not connected with the bear they had tracked for 3 weeks. And they hadn't located any other sign.

Before he left, he talked with me. Though he had hunted all over the world, he had never run into a hunt that so tested his endurance.

This development had a silver lining for me. The hunter's guide, an Indian named Tommy Karcikof, was now available. From reference checks before the hunt, I knew Tommy was Bob's best guide. Tommy won't win an award for friendliness and isn't big on conversation. But he can hunt.

After bidding farewell to the Iowa hunter, Bob's advice to Tommy and me was to forget about the bear they had been tracking. He inhabited an area that apparently made him "unkillable." Tommy didn't like hearing this. His pride was bruised, and he doesn't like to lose.

Taking Bob's advice we headed into another area. We hunted hard for several days, but found no tracks. No sign. Nothing. Just snow, ice and cold.

With long days in the bush, not much food and limited water, my spirits again started to fall. During white-out days when we were trapped in spike camp I started to get "cabin fever." This was a mental struggle.

After a hard day Tommy and I returned to spike camp. With darkness encroaching, neither of us mentioned food or thought about cranking up the stove. Tommy said he needed to think and crawled into his sleeping bag. I did the same.

As I lay there on the snow and ice, I got the feeling that tomorrow Tommy would find that large bear's tracks and give him another try.

At daybreak we made a large break-

Continued ...

fast. Tommy said to eat well. I knew we were in for a long haul. I could see a hint of renewed enthusiasm in this weathered Indian who is the toughest man I've ever met.

I told him I just wanted to see a bear track.

He said, "Trust me."

Around 2:00 that afternoon, far from spike camp, Tommy found the bear's trail. It looked like a small bulldozer had switchbacked up the steep, densely timbered slope. The tracks were huge. I clutched my rifle to assure myself of its readiness.

At the sight of the tracks, my guide was obsessed. It was as if getting this bear meant life or death. He was anxious and intolerant as we followed the day-old tracks. I struggled to stay with him.

Hour after hour the tracks led us through dense stands of spruce, over deadfalls and through deep snow. Exhaustion and dehydration were evident. We each had one 7-ounce container of fruit juice. At about 7 p.m. I drank mine. Whenever the activity slowed or halted I could feel how wet I was from sweat. Tommy said there was a serious danger of hypothermia.

At 8 p.m. we stopped and built a fire to rest and dry out. My hopes of catching this bruin were waning, but our luck was about to change. Shortly after we started back on the trail, the tracks led over a frozen creekbed. Finally it

was easy walking, and we could both make good time!

Farther down the trail we stumbled across a moose kill and fresh grizzly tracks—we had jumped the bear off the carcass!

Tommy knew the area well. I watched his plan unfold as we left the tracks and circled. He wanted to cut the bear off.

As we neared the top of the ridge where the bear was heading I gasped for breath and drew energy from adrenaline. Then Tommy hollered, and I suddenly saw brown movement in a dense spruce thicket. The bear struggled to charge through the thicket to escape.

I had come too far to blow it. The bear would soon disappear into an impenetrable thicket. Three shots rapidly fired from my .338 Win. Mag. and the big bear went down.

I was too tired to feel anything, and I honestly didn't know whether to hug or punch Tommy.

I lay exhausted next to my grizzly bear in the deep snow. Sadness overcame my excitement as I realized the end to the bear's reign over this wilderness.

Tommy had regained his spirit and his confidence. I had redefined my limitations for endurance and had realized one of the greatest accomplishments in North American hunting.

We arrived back at spike camp after

sunrise, roughly 22 hours since our departure the previous morning. Lots of liquids, then a warm sleeping bag were in order.

At base camp, we squared the hide at 9 feet 2 inches. The skull was later measured at $24^0/_{16}$ Boone and Crockett points.

Rifles for Really Big Bears

Grizzly and brown bears are one and the same from a scientific standpoint. It's just that the coastal brown bear lives an easier life and over the years has evolved into a bigger bear. Based on weights, a grizzly is about twice as big as a black bear, and a brown is three times as big. Polar bears are about the same as the brown bear in weight.

All these bears share a common bond in that they are North America's only true dangerous big game. They have the ability, disposition, tools and willingness to kill you. It would serve you well to keep that in mind when selecting a rifle to hunt the big bears.

From the standpoint of what to shoot them with, we can consider these bears as all alike. They are big, tough, nasty tempered and hard to kill. If you hunt them, it will be expensive, and it's unlikely that you will ever do much of it in your lifetime. You owe it to yourself and to the bear to show up well equipped.

The minimum gun suggested in most texts is a .300 magnum with 200-grain bullets. I don't know about you,

but if I were facing 1,000 pounds of raging teeth and claws, .30 caliber would seem pretty puny no matter what the bullet weight.

A .338 Win. Mag. with 250-grain bullets seems like a more prudent minimum to my thinking. Better still, consider the .340 Wthby Mag., .338-378 Wthby Mag. or .338 Rem. Ultra Mag. The .375 H&H Mag. with 270- to 300-grain bullets seems about right, and the .378 Wthby Mag. doesn't look like too much gun to me. Any of the .416 rifles with 400-grain bullets would make decent shooters for big bears.

While many guides carry .458 Win., it's not really a bear hunting cartridge. Guides usually don't bring their rifles into action until things have turned sour. That means they aren't shooting until the bear is too close. When you are hunting, it's foolish to shoot at a bear that's a long way away from you, but with a good rifle a 250-yard shot is reasonable. The .458 Win. is not really a 250-yard gun.

—Bryce Towsley

Mallard Duck

ANAS PLATYRHYNCHOS

OTHER NAMES:

Mallard, greenhead, redlegs

CHARACTERISTICS:

Our most abundant and popular duck. Males (drakes) sport a green head, white ring around the neck, rusty-purple chest and elegant gray-silver belly plumage. The bill is orange or yellow. Hens are mottled brown, lighter on the belly and darker on the back. Females' bills are orange dotted with black.

HABITAT:

Mallards love marshes, sloughs, ponds and other shallow water areas. Agricultural land nearby is an added bonus and will attract a lot of ducks to an area when crops are available for eating. Mallards are tough ducks and will stick around northern climes until water freezes; they will move south only as they need to.

FOOD:

Mallards love grains of all kinds including corn, soybeans, wheat, sorghum, barley and milo. Wild rice, coontail, bulrushes and many other types of aquatic plants are eaten on the water. Look for mallards "tipping" up to get this food, their heads below the surface and their rear ends up in the air.

BEHAVIOR:

Mallards love each others' company, quacking and clucking and purring and generally talking up a big ruckus.

NESTING:

Many drakes will chase a single hen for breeding privileges. The hen will then nest on land but usually within a hundred yards or so of the water, building a nice nest of grass, leaves and twigs. After 28 days of incubating her 8 to 12 eggs, she will lead her brood down to the water. This early trip is a dangerous time for the young ducklings.

HUNTING STRATEGIES:

Set up a good string of decoys, and get everybody in the blind calling to attract passing flocks. Take your camouflage seriously, and don't look up when the birds are coming in or overhead; the movement and your face will cause the ducks to flare off.   —Tom Carpenter

Recipes

Italian Venison Burritos

Ingredients

2 lbs. venison roast
2 tbs. butter
5 large bell peppers
2 medium onions
3 celery ribs
4 cloves garlic

$^1/_4$ tsp. oregano (or to taste)
Salt
Pepper
1 pkg. brown gravy mix
1 pkg. 20-count tortillas

Preparation

Dice venison into $^1/_2$ -inch cubes; sauté in butter until cooked. Dice bell peppers, onions and celery; add to skillet. Cook on low, cover. Crush and dice garlic, add with oregano to skillet. Salt and pepper to taste. Simmer on low until onions and celery are translucent. Add gravy mix and stir until juice thickens. Remove from heat. Spoon into heated tortillas and wrap into burrito style. This dish may be garnished with sour cream, piquant sauce and/or cheese.

Marcus & Rebecca Hanna
Rawlins, WY

TIPS AFIELD

Urban Bowhunter's Code of Conduct

If an urban/suburban community approves a bowhunting program, it's up to each hunter to ensure its long-term success.

* Always hunt as if you're being watched, advises the National Bowhunter Education Foundation. Your actions will speak for all bowhunters, so make it a good message.

* Always put your best foot forward in appearance and conduct, and always be considerate of others.

* Never drink alcohol before or while you are hunting.

* Respect landowners and their land. Meet with them before the season to find out their concerns.

* Find out where the landowner wants you to park your vehicle, where you can hunt and whether the landowner has any special rules. Find out if you can use a treestand and whether/where you can prune shooting lanes. Find out how they want you to remove a deer from their property.

* Leave gates as you found them.

* Know and obey city and state regulations.

- Know where you can take a safe shot and where you can't.

- Take only 100 percent sure shots. It is your responsibility to ensure that no animal will travel far after it's shot.

- To ensure a quick recovery, shoot only when the animal is relaxed and unalert.

- Be patient and wait after the shot. A wounded animal running through a backyard will not score points with anyone.

- When blood-trailing a deer, move cautiously and quietly. Do not take a large group to help recover a deer.

- Mark the blood trail with flagging or toilet tissue, and be sure to remove it before going home.

- If you did not make a good hit, do not give up on the trail until you are certain your shot was not fatal. You, not a nonhunter, must find the game.

- Be discreet on how you remove a deer from the field. This might require moving your vehicle to a more discreet spot, but first get the landowner's approval.

- You might wish to cover the game with a tarp while transporting it from the field. Most people don't like to see a dead animal.

- Bury the entrails deep enough so birds, dogs or other animals cannot find them, or carry them out of the woods in a trash bag.

- If you miss your target, be sure to find the stray arrow.

- Avoid confrontations, no matter the circumstances. Most states have laws against hunter harassment. Don't argue with the antagonist, but report any harassment to the proper authorities.

Ring-Necked Pheasant

GAME PROFILES

PHASIANUS COLCHICUS

OTHER NAMES:

Ringneck, pheasant, rooster

CHARACTERISTICS:

Our most colorful gamebird, a native of the Orient introduced to the U.S. in the 1880s. A rooster or cock (male) sports a bright white ring around a purple-green neck and head; there is a bright red patch of skin (called a wattle) around each eye. The bird's body is an iridescent copper color, with shades of purple and blue. The tail may stream out for up to 2 feet behind him. Hens are a more uniform mottled brown. An adult rooster will weigh $2^1/2$ to 3 pounds, a hen around $1^3/4$ to 2 pounds.

HABITAT:

Pheasants are gamebirds of the open country (agricultural or grassland) with an edge component to it—marshes, fencelines, brushy shelterbelts, woodlots. Grassy cover near the ground is key.

FOOD:

Small grains (which explains the ringneck's love of agricultural areas) and seeds are staples of the diet. When available in summer, insects are important, as are berries and fruits on or near the ground in the late summer and into autumn.

BEHAVIOR:

Pheasants feed for an hour or two in the early morning, then retire to light, grassy loafing cover for the day. After a late afternoon feeding session, the birds move back into heavier roosting cover for the night. Bad weather holds the birds in tough, thick cover all day.

NESTING:

In spring, roosters crow and show off their puffed-up red wattles to attract hens. A hen will go off to lay her 5 to 12 brownish-olive eggs in a shallow bowl scratched out of grassy cover.

HUNTING STRATEGIES:

Smart hunters figure out their local pheasants' routines (see BEHAVIOR section above) and hunt the proper cover at the proper time of day. Walk, walk, walk until you find the birds. A good dog is almost a must for tracking down and retrieving downed birds. You'll also flush more birds with a good dog. Pheasants are notorious runners, reluctant to take wing.

—Tom Carpenter

TIPS AFIELD

Tips for Sighting in Your Rifle

You may encounter 250-yard shots while hunting, but the only range available to you for sighting in your rifle is 50 yards. How can you sight in?

Joe Ventimiglia of Venco Industries has the answer.

"Set up your target at 25 yards for a scoped rifle, 12.5 yards for one with iron sights. The short yardage makes spotting and adjustments easy—and at the same time you are approximating where the bullet will strike the same target if it were 200 to 300 yards down range."

"In most hunting calibers, where a bullet 'prints' at 25 yards will roughly be where it prints at 220 to 230 yards. Because your sights or scope are mounted on top of the barrel, above the line of sight, your gun is positioned to shoot slightly upward to compensate. The bullet leaves the bore in such a manner that it actually rises above the sight line, travels in an arc and drops back below the sight line as gravity works on it down range."

"Ballistic charts show, for example, that a scope-sighted .270 firing 130-grain factory loads at about 3,100 feet per second, zeroed at 25 yards, will group 3 inches high at 100 yards, 4 inches high at 200 and dead-on at 275. A similarly scoped .30-06 shooting 150-grain factory loads at 2,700 feet per second zeroed at 25 yards will be almost 3 inches high at 100, a bit over 2 inches at 200 and back at the point of aim at 250 yards."

"The gun should be fine-tuned at 100 yards, but the shorter range sighting will get you close if that's all that is available. One caution: When you sight in a rifle, the resultant accuracy pattern is good only for that exact configuration of scope or sight, load and bullet type. Any change in sight height, load or bullet type will grossly exaggerate differences down range."

MOOSE

HUNTER:
Dale Brewster

RESIDENCE:
Stanley, North Dakota

WHERE TAKEN:
Alberta, Canada

ARMS USED:
Browning .338 Mag Rifle

Dale was hunting with Doig River outfitters of Fairview, Alberta.

What Does Caliber Mean?

The word "caliber" simply refers to the rough diameter of a rifle or pistol bore, measured in divisions of an inch or in millimeters.

Technically, in the United States and England, a caliber is $^1/_{100}$ of an inch. A 30-caliber bore, therefore, is $^{30}/_{100}$ of an inch. A 270-caliber bore measures $^{27}/_{100}$ of an inch. Decimal points are commonly used when referring to calibers—.30 caliber, .270 caliber—but that is technically incorrect, says Joe Ventimiglia, shooting expert and gun-care product manufacturer.

"In all other countries caliber is measured in millimeters. Some metric measurements are very close to their Anglo counterparts. Generally speaking, you can match the size of a metric caliber to one measured in inches by multiplying by 4. For example, a 6-millimeter bore equates to 24 caliber, which is the American .243; the 7-millimeter equates to our .280. The Japanese 7.7 matches our .308, but the Russian-Chinese 7.62 is slightly larger than our 30 caliber when multiplied by 4."

Black Bear

URSUS AMERICANUS

OTHER NAMES:

American black bear, cinnamon bear

CHARACTERISTICS:

Coat can be black (often with white on chest), brown or blond; slight shoulder hump, but highest point of body above hips; muzzle straight and long in profile; claws on front feet dark, strongly curved and shorter (seldom more than $1^1/2$ inches) than those of grizzly; males weigh 180 to 250 pounds, occasionally up to 400 pounds; females weigh 120 to 180 pounds.

HABITAT:

Dense forests, riparian areas; open slopes or avalanche chutes during spring green-up.

FOOD:

Grasses, sedges, berries, fruits, inner bark of trees, insects, honey, eggs, carrion, rodents, occasional ungulates (especially young and domestic) and garbage (where available).

BEHAVIOR:

Largely nocturnal; usually solitary; dig less elaborate dens than grizzlies, often in natural cavities (trees, rocks), under logs, brush piles or even buildings; climb trees easily.

REPRODUCTION:

Similar to grizzlies, except females often first breed at $2^1/2$ or $3^1/2$ years of age; in very poor habitat, may not breed until $6^1/2$ years of age.

HUNTING:

Done over bait where legal. But in the West, spot-and-stalk hunting is common.

GAME BIRDS: PHEASANTS

NAME:
John Newbanks

RESIDENCE:
Concord, CA

WHERE TAKEN:
Birds Landing, California

ARMS USED:
Browning Citori; Remington Field
Loads

*No. 7 1/2 shot was enough lead for John
and his companion, Bret, to bring home
these pheasants.*

NAME:
Andy Hollenback

RESIDENCE:
Epworth, IA

WHERE TAKEN:
Iowa

*Andy and his Chesapeake retriever, Ruby, and their
daily limit of three Iowa cock pheasants.*

Hunt Safely with Your Dog

Bob West, dog trainer and consultant, has key suggestions for safe hunting with your gun dog:

- As you walk, make a habit of checking that the safety of your gun is on.
- Keep the muzzle pointed up.
- If a dog goes on point, move into the area carefully, from the side if possible, so he can see you coming.
- Note your partner's position. Aggressively flush the bird to get it flying. Many hunters take turns, deciding who will flush and who will shoot before the shot.
- Only shoot birds that fly high and clear of hunters and dogs. Never shoot at low flyers. An unsteady pointer or flushing dog may jump in the air after a low bird.
- Don't shoot crippled birds on the ground. Hunting dogs are trained to track and retrieve cripples. A fast-walking dog can seemingly come from nowhere after a cripple and could easily be shot in the process.
- After shooting, return your safety to the "on" position.
- Be alert to signals of fatigue. Slowed tail action or a tail being carried lower is a sign of fatigue. Other signs are panting, an anxious expression and darker red color of the gums. When these symptoms appear, back off. Allow the dog to rest and cool down.
- Put a collar of hunter-orange coloration on your dog.
- Know your partner's location at all times.
- At the end of the hunt, unload your guns before calling the dogs to heel. Back at the vehicle, hold your partner's gun while he puts the dogs in their crates. Take time to check the dogs' general condition. Look for cuts, burrs or thorns.

After the Shot

*O*ften, most of the time spent on a big game archery hunt is prior to the shot. What a bowhunter does after the shot, however, may be crucial to recovering his game and getting it back to camp. Successfully tracking a wounded game animal requires knowledge, patience and, sometimes, a lot of time. The following questions are adapted from information provided by the National Bowhunter Education Foundation. See if your instincts agree with the recommendations of the foundation by answering these True or False questions.

1 After the shot, stay put. Don't immediately begin to track your deer.

2 Wounded deer usually run with their tail up.

3 Wait at least 6 hours before starting to trail an animal hit in the guts, weather and circumstances permitting.

4 Gut shot animals often "hump" their back when hit.

5 When tracking a wounded animal with a companion, speak loudly to keep tabs on each other's location.

6 When trailing wounded game, follow its trail precisely, walking exactly where it did.

7 If no more blood sign shows on the trail, you can end your search, knowing you gave it a thorough effort until the blood sign ended.

8 Birds can be an asset in tracking wounded game.

9 Vitally hit animals often go downhill rather than climb.

10 Gut shot animals become thirsty and often go toward water.

Answers

1 True. Stay put and try to remember where the hit was made on the animal. With binoculars try to identify some landmark to aid in locating the correct trail it took to escape.

2 False. Wounded deer usually run with their tail down.

3 True. Gut shot animals almost always die from the wound.

4 True.

5 False. Trail very quietly. Avoid talking. Use hand signals or soft whistles to communicate with a companion.

6 False. Be careful not to disturb the animals trail and sign that it left behind, by staying just to the side of the trail.

7 False. Make sure the last blood sign is conspicuously marked with surveyor tape, crepe paper or toilet tissue, and from that point check all main trail lanes or trails for at least half a mile.

8 True. If no blood or animal can be found, but you feel the hit was a lethal one, sit down and listen. Often crows, ravens, magpies or jays will be attracted to a downed animal. Listen for their calls.

9 True.

10 True.

Deer's keen Senses

*T*he deer has keen senses of smell, sight and hearing. Here are suggestions from Pete Rickard, scent and call manufacturer, on how to best combat those senses.

Smell

Keep your body and clothes clean and free from all foreign odors. Avoid using scented soaps, shampoos, laundry detergents and fabric softeners. Don't use a clothes dryer; residual odors will probably be present. Never wear your hunting boots at a gas station or your own garage. Never pump your own gas. Never fill the gas tank before you hunt; fumes and odors will seep into your vehicle and stick to your clothes and body. Never smoke, drink or chew tobacco during the hunt.

Hearing

Always wear quiet clothing. Ensure the stability of your treestand, so it won't creak with every movement. Clear leaves and twigs from areas and paths you plan to walk through regularly. Be careful not to spook other wildlife, such as birds and squirrels, which could give you away by their chattering.

Vision

Always hunt with something behind you like a large tree trunk, stone wall, foliage or brush. If the background is low, kneel down to cover your outline. Never hunt from ridges or hills that cause the sky to outline your shape. Don't blink until after you've released the bowstring or squeezed the trigger.

Mule Deer

ODOCOILEUS HEMIONUS

OTHER NAMES:
Blacktail, black-tailed deer (fairly common but confusing because two smaller species of mule deer along the West Coast are called blacktails)

CHARACTERISTICS:
Coat gray in winter, brownish in summer; forehead and brisket dark; chin, throat and rump patch white; tail short and round with black tip; ears large (reason for name); antlers fork and fork again; typical adult buck has four tines on each side (or five if brow tines are present); brow tines are shorter than those of whitetails or may be absent; outside of hind foot has slit-like scent gland up to 7 inches long; mature bucks weigh 170 to 250 pounds on good range, does 140 to 180 pounds.

HABITAT:
Grasslands interspersed with brushy coulees or breaks; riparian habitat along prairie rivers; open to dense mountain and coniferous forests, aspen groves.

FOOD:
Bitterbrush, mountain mahogany, chokecherry, serviceberry, sagebrush, grasses and forbs. Crops where available.

BEHAVIOR:
More gregarious and migratory (mostly elevational movements) than white-tailed deer; feed early and late in the day; run with tail down in bounding leaps, keeping all four feet together.

REPRODUCTION:
Breed in late November; one or two grayish but white-spotted fawns; bucks gather harems; necks of rutting bucks swell; healthy adult bucks shed antlers in December and January; does usually breed first as yearlings (16 to 17 months).

HUNTING:
Mule deer hunting is often a spot-and-stalk scenario. Their habitat is so big, you usually have to move around to find the deer, then sneak into position for a shot.

Dog First Aid

BY GLENN SAPIR

Check your dog's eyes for seeds and other debris periodically during the hunt and at the end of each day.

When afield with your dog, medical emergencies may occur that you must be equipped to handle. Here is valuable advice from dog trainer and Ralston Purina consultant Bob West:

Don't underestimate a bruise or closed wound. If your dog is in pain, and if you see swelling along with a warm feel to the injured area, see a veterinarian as soon as possible. In the meantime, clean the area with cold water and apply ice packs.

Open wounds are more serious. Substantial blood loss can be life threatening. Left unattended, infection can cause complications. At the very

least, pain and swelling can put your dog out of action for several days. See a vet as soon as possible.

Check your dog when switching fields at the end of the day. Look for small cuts or scratches, clean them with antiseptic soap, then apply a topical antibiotic ointment that your vet has recommended. If possible, see your veterinarian within 24 hours.

For severe wounds or those involving considerable blood loss, your primary responsibility is to control the bleeding and stabilize the dog's condition while he or she is being transported to professional care. Apply a pressure bandage to the wounded area. A pressure bandage is some type of padding, such as gauze pads, applied directly on the wound, either by hand or kept in place with tape. Use enough pressure to stop bleeding, yet not so tight as to stop circulation.

Broken bones most often involve the leg. Usually the leg hangs unnaturally, the dog won't put any weight on it or he shows extreme lameness. Muzzle your dog gently with a flat strip of cloth or gauze or a commercial muzzle. Loop the material over the nose just behind the canine teeth, catching the lower jaw. Bring the ends down under and make a half-hitch to hold the jaws together. Bring the ends around the neck below the ears and tie it off in a bow knot behind his head.

Once your dog is muzzled, keep him quiet and handle him gently. Do not attempt to splint bones. Instead, support the leg in some way to avoid further damage while transporting. A loosely wrapped towel or sweatshirt will do the job. In the case of compound fractures, where the broken bone has punctured the skin, stop the bleeding by covering the wound. Keep it as clean as possible. Get your dog to the nearest vet as soon as possible.

Serious injury and severe trauma can result from an accident such as being hit by a car. In these cases, broken bones and open wounds can be minor problems compared to the probability of internal bleeding and shock. Never pick up the dog by the waist or chest. You could force a broken rib through a lung or organ. Put a rug or blanket on the ground behind the dog and drag him onto it by the loose skin of his neck and back. Then, you and another person can lift the dog to safety using the rug as a stretcher. You may need to remuzzle your dog to do this. Be sure he can breathe, especially if the injuries are to the head, face or neck.

Check to see that the airway is clear.

Pull the tongue out and to the side, check for blood or other material and clear the mouth and throat. Talk quietly to your injured dog to help keep him calm. Quickly take measures to control bleeding and otherwise prepare the dog for immediate transportation to a vet. If the chest cavity is punctured, you will hear a sucking sound at the wound as air goes in and out. Seal it so the dog can breathe. Cover the area with a cloth, applying pressure until the noise stops, then wrap with tape. If there's an object protruding from the hole, leave it for your veterinarian to remove. Never give the dog food or water while he is being transported. Cover him to maintain body heat as a measure against shock.

Shock may be defined as a lack of adequate blood flow to meet the body's needs. The body tries to correct this loss by speeding up the heart, constricting peripheral blood vessels and conserving fluid in circulation to more central parts of the body. If allowed to continue, vital organs begin to shut down for lack of oxygen. Shock then becomes self-perpetuating and can cause death.

Symptoms are a drop in body temperature, lethargy, cold extremities, pale gums and mucus membranes and a rapid, but weak pulse. Once diagnosed, remove the cause if possible. Calm the dog and help him assume a comfortable position. Cover him with a blanket while transporting him for help.

Continued ...

Heat stress shows early symptoms, such as less body activity and increased panting. As the problem becomes more evident, you'll see aggravated panting, salivation, a panicky expression; the gums become dark red and the dog has problems with coordination. Your primary goal is to reduce body temperature. Flush his mouth with cool water to remove saliva. Immerse the dog in cool water if possible, or use wet rags, ice packs or available water to cool the under parts, ears and tongue. Cooling these areas reduces the temperature of the circulating blood, which helps to cool the body core. If possible, take your dog immediately to a vet.

Eye care is important. Check your dog's eyes periodically during the hunt or at least at the end of the day. Weed seeds and debris can become lodged under the lids and cause irritation or even corneal ulcers, which are painful. By carefully spreading the upper and lower lids you can see the entire eye. Pay special attention to the "third eyelid"; it's actually a second low lid, and the inside corners are likely places for trapped debris. If debris is present, try flushing it free with a stream of sterile isotonic saline. If that doesn't work, try to blot it out with a cotton ball soaked in sterile isotonic saline. DON'T WIPE. BLOT SOFTLY. Wiping can scratch the eye, causing more damage. When the eye is cleared, check with your veterinarian. Sometimes the object gets lodged behind the third eyelid, which usually requires a vet's attention.

Canine First-Aid kit

ORGANIZE THE FOLLOWING IN A SMALL TACKLE BOX:

- ❑ Roll of gauze
- ❑ Forceps
- ❑ Gauze pads
- ❑ Sterile isotonic saline & dispenser
- ❑ Roll of adhesive tape
- ❑ Cotton balls
- ❑ Betadine scrub
- ❑ Cotton swabs
- ❑ Betadine ointment
- ❑ Rectal thermometer
- ❑ Scissors
- ❑ Steroid-free ophthalmic antibiotic
- ❑ Toenail clipper ointment

Water for Your Dogs

"One cannot emphasize enough the importance of fresh drinking water for dogs in all kinds of weather," says Dr. Dave Bebiak of Ralston Purina.

Water is one of the most important nutrients dogs require. Because a dog's body has a limited capacity to store water, life may continue for weeks in the absence of food but only for days when water is not available, Bebiak explains.

Water constitutes up to 84 percent of the weight of newborn puppies and 50 to 60 percent of the weight of adult dogs. Water helps to regulate body temperature, cushion the joints and internal organs, digest food, eliminate waste, lubricate tissue and allow salt and electrolytes to pass through the body.

"This is why fresh drinking water in a clean bowl should be available to your hunting dog at all times," Bebiak stresses.

If you find yourself without a bowl but have some aluminum foil, even from the wrapper of a sandwich, you can fashion a bowl out of the foil.

BLACK BEARS

NAME:
Jim Wilson

RESIDENCE:
Apollo, PA

WHERE TAKEN:
New Mexico

ARMS USED:
Golden Eagle Splitfire 1
Bow; Bloodtrailer III
Broadheads

Joel was hunting with Bear Facts Outfitters when he got his black bear.

NAME:
Joe Biltz

RESIDENCE:
Brookville, IN

WHERE TAKEN:
Liverpool, Nova Scotia,
Canada

ARMS USED:
Remington 700 .30-06
Rifle; Federal Ballistic Tip
Bullets

A Hairy Approach to Tracking Wounded Whitetails

A knowledge of hair distribution on a white-tailed deer can aid you in trailing a wounded deer. Knowing where you hit the deer can help you determine the extent of its injuries. The National Bowhunters Education Foundation notes these distinctions:

- Back hair is long, dark (often black-tipped) and coarse.

- Neck hair is like short back hair except underneath, or at the front of the neck, where it is short and light colored.

- Brisket hair is very dark and twisted near the junction of the neck and the body.

- Side hair is short and brown, with dark tips.

- The hair at the bottom of the rib cage is a mixture of white and dark brown hairs, moderately long and thick.

- The belly hair tends to be white, long, fine and sometimes twisted.

- Tail hair is very long. The top of the tail is dark brown, with hair tipped with black.

- The rear of the ham or flank is where the belly hairs and long, dark brown side hairs meet. Lower legs have very short reddish-brown hair.

Rabbit Gumbo

Meat

2 rabbits (3 to 4 lbs. each) cut
  into 8 pieces
6 garlic cloves, crushed
1 bayleaf

2 tbs. Paul Prudhomme
  Seafood Magic
  Seasoning Blend
1 cup white wine

Combine all ingredients in a non-reactive (stainless steel or ceramic) bowl and marinate 24 hours. Drain rabbit and discard marinade. Heat 4 tbs. corn oil in an 8-qt. stockpot. Pat rabbit pieces dry; sear the pieces quickly in oil until golden brown. Drain on paper towels and discard the oil.

Stock

Browned rabbit pieces
1 onion, chopped
1 bell pepper, chopped
3 ribs celery, chopped

4 cloves garlic, minced
1 bunch parsley
6 sprigs thyme
3-qts. chicken stock

Place all ingredients in stockpot and bring to a boil. Reduce heat and simmer 2-3 hours until rabbit is tender. Remove the pieces and set aside. Strain stock, discarding the vegetables and reserve. Strip and save; discard bones.

Gumbo

6 tbs. butter
6 tbs. flour
1 large onion, diced
1 red bell pepper, diced
1 green bell pepper, diced
4 ribs celery, sliced
8 cloves garlic, minced
8 green onions, chopped fine
1 jalapeño pepper minced fine
1 habanero pepper left whole

1 cup white wine
2 qts. Rabbit stock (more if
   necessary)
1 tbs. Worcestershire sauce
1 tsp. Tabasco sauce
2 tbs. Paul Prudhomme
   Seafood Magic
   Seasoning Blend
1/2 cup parsley chopped
Reserved rabbit meat

Melt butter in stockpot; add flour and stir. Lower heat to medium, and stir until mixture is a deep chocolate color.

Stir in onions, bell peppers, celery, garlic and jalapeño and habanero peppers. Bring to a rapid boil; lower heat and simmer one hour. Add reserved rabbit meat. Season with salt and pepper. Serve over rice or mashed potatoes.

Albert Bottari
Richmond Hill, NY

ALL IN FUN

THE FINE ART OF FIBBING

BY JIM SHOCKEY

"**Y**ou lied! You told me you got your bear up the left fork of Shaw Creek."

"I did not ... er ... lie, I mean."

Billy was at my door accusing me.

"Yes you did ... er ... lie, I mean."

I had to make a decision: come clean or play dumb?

"Did I say the left fork?" I scratched my head. "Well, you know the hill with the tree on it and the bridge on the other side and then the road cuts to the left? Is that the fork or is the fork up higher and toward the river where the water runs between the two big boulders? I'm confused, but wasn't he a Granddaddy bear?"

Rule #1: Clean is what you do to fish. Dumb is what you do to other hunters trying to find your secret hot spot.

"Don't play dumb," Bill Shook his head sadly. "Two of my buddies watched you through spotting scopes."

I almost flinched. *Fact* is the worst enemy of the hunter playing dumb.

Rule #2: Fact is bad, but it's no match for a good bluff.

"Ha! Caught you, liar!" He smiled and stuck out his chest. "They weren't up there, they were way down in the valley."

"Right. Way down in the valley when they saw me, but way up at the start of the valley when I saw them. Figured those clowns couldn't see worth beans."

Rule #3: Discredit the prosecution's witness.

"Probably didn't see my truck until they were right on top of it." I assumed if his buddies had seen me, they could not have missed my 4X4.

"Truck? What truck? You told me you backpacked in."

Rule #4: Never offer the enemy any information until you are sure he already has it.

I was in serious trouble. I had told Billy I backpacked 10 miles up to the head of Shaw Creek in the morning, bagged my bear and then packed it out before dark. The road that leads up to Shaw Creek has a locked gate on it. Unless you know the mythical 4X4 back way into the valley, it's a long uphill hike. I winced and turned my head away from what I knew would be coming.

"How could you?" The hurt was obvious in his voice.

I was in the presence of a master. Even my wife could not have said it better. She would have thrown in a few tears for effect, but not Billy. He was smiling like a warden with a warrant to search a poacher's freezer.

"You told me you didn't know the back way in." He was gloating. "You said you wanted me to show you."

Suddenly the leer faded from his face as the fact of the matter became clear. If I had my 4X4 up the valley, then it was obvious I had discovered the mythical back way into the valley. For Billy, who was the only living soul reputed to know the back way in, the fact that I also now knew was devastating.

The world brightened as I watched Billy's claim to fame slip from his grasp. I smiled to myself. He forgot rule number 5.

Rule #5: Never jump to conclusions.

"Actually," I paused, checking the nails of my hand with disinterest, "I don't know the back way into the valley."

Rule #6: Used sparingly, the truth can be a very effective way to lie.

"You don't?" He grasped for the tiny bit of hope I had thrown him.

"Nope."

"How'd you get in with your truck then?"

"Through the gate."

"No way." Even though he faced going through life without friends, he would not let himself believe that I had somehow managed to get my hands on "The Key."

Every local hunter knew "The Key" existed. It had to, at least one copy. Legend had the key made of gold and hanging, like a priceless icon, on the wall in the office of the president of the huge timber company owning the rights to log Shaw Creek.

"Yes, Bill," I placed a hand on his shoulder, "I'm afraid it's the truth. I've got 'The Key.' I swear on my honor."

Continued ...

111

"Where'd you get it?"

"I can't tell."

"Yeah, and I have the key to Buckingham Palace." He was beginning to regain his composure. "I don't believe you."

It was time to play my ace in the hole. "Our good friend Tom gave it to me." I smiled sweetly. "He said I was not supposed to tell you because you would tell the whole world."

"Not tell me? That jerk!"

I had implemented rule 7.

Rule #7: When the going gets tough, do not be afraid to sacrifice a friend's honor to save your own.

"Where did he get the key?"

"He really is a jerk."

"Yep."

"And a liar."

"The worst." I agreed and motioned for my vanquished foe to come in the house. "Thirsty?"

"Sure."

We walked to my trophy room.

"Who was it that saw me up Shaw Creek anyway?" I asked.

"Oh that. I just made that up to see if you really did get your bear there."

"No kidding?" I frowned. "I thought so."

"Why's that?" Billy asked.

"I've never been up Shaw Creek." I answered. "I only said I got my bear there to see if you know a way in."

"Clever. But where did you get your bear then?"

"Shaw Creek."

"I knew it all along."

We toasted each other.

Did You Know?

Did you know that a baby powder bottle with seven or eight small holes in the top and filled with foot powder sends out a nice cloud that you can easily track as it wafts away. This will let you know where deer are likely to get your wind and helps you plan when and where you'll need to shoot a deer in order to avoid being smelled first.

ELK

SOMETHING TO SHOOT FOR

HUNTER:
Jack Lamson

RESIDENCE:
Albany, Vermont

WHERE TAKEN:
Youngsville, New Mexico

ARMS USED:
Remington Model 700
.30-06 Rifle; Safari-Grade
Ammo With an A-Frame
Bullet

Jack made the most of the elk hunt he won during an NAHC membership drive. He hunted with Robert Davis Jr., outfitter and guide for Southwestern Outfitters & Guides out of Albuquerque.

HUNTER:
Michael Pevine

RESIDENCE:
Salisbury, New Hampshire

WHERE TAKEN:
Utah

ARMS USED:
.300 Winchester Mag Rifle

Michael was hunting with Pine Ranch Outfitters.

One Pain of a Pronghorn

BY JEFF WYCKOFF

FAVORITE HUNTS

Drawing a pronghorn permit in Arizona's Unit 10 wasn't easy. It usually took years. I'd been trying unsuccessfully for 20. But my father, Don Wyckoff, finally beat the odds.

Actually, drawing the permit turned out to be the easiest part of this hunt for my dad.

Anyone who knows pronghorns, especially trophy-class bucks, also understands that Arizona is the place to take a Boone and Crockett Club buck. As a result, demand was high for the limited number of permits. Despite filling out applications for nearly 30 years, this was only Dad's second permit. The one he had drawn almost 20 years earlier had gone unfilled.

Almost 20 years older and slowed by an artificial knee, Dad faced even stiffer odds in filling his tag. We both knew this was probably his last chance to take a trophy pronghorn.

Being a full-time guide and outfitter here in Arizona, I'd had the opportunity to guide clients for deer and pronghorn in Unit 10. I'd also had archery pronghorn permits for that unit, so I had a good idea where to begin our preseason scouting.

During a scouting trip in mid-August, I had located an exceptional buck and was fortunate enough to videotape him with his harem of does. A few days later, after viewing the video with my father, we decided to devote the entire season to taking this particular buck.

Opening morning, with the stars shining brightly, we left the vehicle with more than an hour to go before daylight and started our hike to the top of the ridge where we hoped to spot the herd of pronghorns with the buck we had come to call "Our Buck."

Because of Dad's artificial knee, we moved slowly and cautiously over the rough, rocky terrain. Daylight found us comfortably in position and glassing the country below. Despite a couple hours of concentrated looking, we were unable to spot the herd of pronghorns that held Our Buck.

We decided to move to another hill that would allow us to glass a different area that the buck and his does sometimes used. This habitat, by the way, isn't your usual pronghorn terrain. It's rolling hills with small openings. There are places where dense juniper and pinion trees are separated by steep ridges etched with rimrock and cliff rose. It looks more like mule deer country.

After lunch and a short break to rest his knee, my father and I started hiking uphill to our next vantage point. Shortly after we reached the destination, we spotted him. Our Buck and his harem of does were about a half-mile away in a small valley. And they were feeding toward us. We quickly formulated a plan that would allow us to stalk into position for a shot. Sneaking across the rough and broken terrain was slow and painful for my father, but we managed to arrive at our ambush spot before the pronghorns did.

As we settled in, we could see the pronghorns inching closer at about 400 yards. Every now and then we could spy Our Buck bringing up the rear of the herd as the animals filtered between trees. Even though the pronghorns were now getting close enough for a shot, Dad didn't want to shoot until he was confident he could make a clean kill.

Finally, the animals at the front of the herd were approximately 200 yards out. All we needed was for Our Buck to step clear. Suddenly, two

distant shots rang out about a quarter mile up the valley. Another hunter had fired at a buck in a different herd of pronghorns and, in the process, sent Our Buck and his does bolting back the way they had come. Dad and I just sat there not knowing what to say or do while watching all of our hard work disappear.

Back at camp we discussed our options and strategies for the next day. We decided to return to the same spot from where we had spotted Our Buck the afternoon before. He didn't show all morning, so in the afternoon we returned to our opening morning spot. Again, Our Buck was nowhere to be found.

The third day was a repeat of the second, and now the miles and heat were starting to wear on my father and me. Dad was beginning to have some problems with swelling around his knee.

Continued ...

115

On day four we trekked to where we had last seen Our Buck that first afternoon. Shortly after sunrise we glassed a buck that we hadn't seen before. This one deserved a better look. He was about a mile away, and after a slow, cautious stalk, we were within 300 yards. Even though he was a very nice buck, we decided to pass on him for now since we still had almost 3 days remaining to hunt for Our Buck.

Returning to our original spot, we sat to glass and eat lunch. After about an hour, a herd of pronghorns appeared moving downhill through the thick cover toward the valley. Bringing up the rear was Our Buck. He was busy keeping two smaller bucks away and seemed to be paying close attention to one of the does. We stayed where we were and observed him for more than an hour as we tried to figure out the best approach.

Dad told me that this would likely be his last stalk, because the pain and swelling around his knee were getting progressively worse. The herd was approximately a mile away. To complicate things even more, two smaller herds of pronghorns were between us. With about 2 hours of daylight left, we started our stalk after locating some landmarks to aid us in finding Our Buck when we got closer.

The first part of the stalk went smoothly but slowly. Our biggest concern was that our herd of pronghorns would move off before we could reach them. Soon we were in sight of the first herd and moved only when their heads were down or when they were screened by trees. Luckily, we managed to sneak by them undetected.

Somehow, we also slipped unnoticed past the second herd. So far, so good.

As I eased slowly through the trees I was startled to see 2 pronghorns walking toward us. Our Buck! They were just 150 yards off. We froze, and as soon as the animals appeared, they changed course and vanished into the trees. We waited for Our Buck to reappear. Twice we caught a glimpse of him moving across the small opening in front of us, but he would either cross too quickly or be screened by other pronghorns.

After not seeing him for about 5 minutes, we were beginning to get nervous. Than a doe stepped into the clearing and brought Our Buck with her. They were coming right toward us! At approximately 100 yards they turned slightly to our right. At that instant, Dad fired. Our Buck collapsed.

After dinner at camp that night, we put a tape to Our Buck's horns and realized that he would easily qualify for the Boone and Crockett record book. What a hunt! I hope that when I finally draw my Unit 10 pronghorn tag, my father will be able to accompany me.

TIPS AFIELD

Dead Deer Talk

By examining the deer you've tagged, you can learn a lot about him, according to Pete Rickard, the scent and call manufacturer.

- Hooves that are hard, chipped, cracked and dry indicate that the deer was a ridge runner or lived beneath ledges.

- Bleached white racks usually indicate that the buck was receiving a lot of sunshine.

- Digested, semi-digested and undigested food in the stomach may be able to help you piece together a travel pattern.

- Ears that are ripped, cracked or torn indicate that this buck had been in a lot of fights. This means that he may be one of the dominant bucks in that area.

- If his rack is small, it may be time to change your hunting location. It may suggest that poor nutrition and genes don't allow for the growth of big antlers.

ELK

HUNTER:
Kenneth Wayne Greene

RESIDENCE:
Leesburg, GA

WHERE TAKEN:
Colorado

ARMS USED:
Remington .300 Mag Rifle

Kenneth was hunting with Pat Grieve of Snake River Outfitters on the Gold Blossom Ranch.

BREATHE EASY

Barrel movement as slight as .003 inch, which is equal to the diameter of a human hair, can move a rifle's point of impact nearly ¼ inch at 100 yards.

Though you probably won't miss your game because of such a slight deviation, you can improve your shooting by cutting down the factors that cause barrel movement.

"The movement caused by simple breathing is one of the biggest factors in barrel and sight movement in shooting," says accuracy expert Frank Ventimiglia. "Controlling your breathing is one big hurdle in achieving accuracy potential with a specific firearm.

"After you are in position and have established the sight picture, take a full breath, slowly let half out, stop and squeeze the trigger. It takes some practice, but it is guaranteed to make you steadier."

Sharp-Tailed Grouse

GAME PROFILES

TYMPANUCHUS PHASIANELLUS

OTHER NAMES:

Sharptail, sharpy, sharky, grouse, prairie grouse

CHARACTERISTICS:

The grouse of wide-open places. Cocks and hens are virtually indistinguishable most of the year. The entire plumage is mottled with brown, gray, beige and black, getting increasingly white down below. The tail is pointed, hence the bird's name. If you ever get a sharptail, examine the feet; they're feathered to the toe! An adult bird will weigh 2 pounds, maybe even a little more.

HABITAT:

Open grasslands and brushlands are a necessity. Good mixtures of croplands, year-round grassland, wooded shelterbelts and rough, broken country (to escape to) makes a perfect sharptail combination. You will find them west of their Great Plains strongholds too, in sagebrush country.

FOOD:

Grains, clover, dandelions, grass seeds; tree and shrub buds, fruits and berries when available; and insects in the summer and early fall.

BEHAVIOR:

Sharptails will travel a long way, if need be, between roosting areas and feeding areas, back to loafing cover and then again back to feeding and then roosting areas. These birds will fly where they need to go, sometimes several miles! You'll usually find sharptails in loose groups of 5 to 15 birds.

NESTING:

The male sharptail's breeding display is impressive. He'll perform a fluttering, jumping dance, along with the other males of the area, on the dancing ground or lek. If a female shows interest, a cock will court her by strutting and cooing to her with his bright yellow eyebrows and purple cheek sacs inflated, then breed. She will lay 8 to 15 buffy eggs in a small depression in brushy cover nearby.

HUNTING STRAGETIES:

Hunt the edges between grassland and cropland, grassland and brushland, or grassland and sage land. Figure out where the birds are feeding (open a bird's crop to look if you get one) and work that cover in early morning or evening. If the weather is wet or very cold, look for brush. Otherwise, stay out in the open areas.

—Tom Carpenter

SOMETHING TO SHOOT FOR

PRONGHORN

NAME:
Willard F. Baird

RESIDENCE:
Warsaw, OH

WHERE TAKEN:
Gillette, Wyoming

ARMS USED:
Savage Model 111 .30-06
Rifle

Willard was hunting with Seven J Outfitters, out of Sundance, Wyoming.

NAME:
Glenn E. Johnson

RESIDENCE:
Clovis, NM

WHERE TAKEN:
New Mexico

ARMS USED:
Rifle; Combine Technology
Silver Tip

Glenn was hunting with guide Ron Troyer at the NRA Whittington Center.

Pronghorn

ANTILOCAPRA AMERICANA

OTHER NAMES:

Antelope, pronghorn antelope

CHARACTERISTICS:

Coat rich russet-tan with white underside; large white rump patch; two white bands across throat; black markings on head; dew claws absent; horns of adult bucks 13 to 17 inches long with prongs and curved tips; horn sheaths shed annually; about 70% of adult does have horns (averaging $1^{1}/_{2}$ inches long); adult bucks weigh 125 pounds, does 110 pounds.

HABITAT:

Open, rolling sagebrush/grasslands.

FOOD:

Forbs and grasses in spring and

summer; sagebrush and other browse all year but especially in winter.

BEHAVIOR:

Adult bucks territorial from March through September; does and fawns in small herds drift on and off bucks' territories in spring and summer; herds of bachelor bucks excluded from territories; all ages and both sexes congregate in winter herds. During severe winters, herds drift for long distances seeking food. Barriers to these movements, such as fences, limit populations. Excited animals emit explosive snorts, erect white rump patches and emit musky odor from glands in rump patches.

REPRODUCTION:

Breed in September and early October; two grayish-brown fawns; bucks fight viciously and sometimes fatally; territorial bucks hold harems to breed; bucks shed horn sheaths in November; females usually breed when $1^{1}/_{2}$ years old, but may breed as fawns.

HUNTING:

With archery gear, sit at a water hole or try a decoy to lure an aggressive buck into range. With rifle, get out of your truck and sneak, peek and stalk your way about the prairie.

Turkey Fight!

TEXT AND PHOTO BY LANCE KRUEGER

Scraping the chalked-up paddle of my box call to mimic an excited hen turkey, my sequence was cut short by an approaching gobbler somewhere in front of us. Two friends, having never seen nor heard a wild turkey, sat on either side of me totally covered in borrowed camouflage to blend in with the South Texas brush. Even my weapon of choice that morning, a Canon camera and 300mm telephoto lens, was covered with camouflage.

Just when I felt the Rio Grande gobbler was about to step into the opening in front of us, I unexpectedly heard the "spit-drum" of a different gobbler going to full strut at close range to our left. Slowly moving my head toward the sound, I saw a different gobbler at full strut with a subordinate jake at 15 yards. Earlier, we had heard him gobble once far behind us, but he seemed less excited than the bird to our front. This pair had beaten the excited gobbler in a footrace by only seconds.

Making his entrance at the edge of the brush, the excited gobbler turned from lover to fighter when he saw he had lost the race. The longbeards immediately walked toward each other with an unmistakable, aggressive demeanor. A crescendo of aggressive purring and gobbling began as the birds approached each other. They bumped chests at 40 yards from our ringside seat. Circling with their left wings nearly touching as challenging gladiators once did, the equally matched rivals tried to show who was bigger and tougher.

I started firing my camera at them as they began to flail each other with their wings and peck at each others' heads. A couple dozen times they jumped simultaneously into the air and beat each other with their wings, each stabbing his enemy with his $1\frac{1}{2}$-inch-long spurs. When they landed back on earth, the combatants would push each other with their chests in a shoving match as they vied for position.

After three minutes of pummeling each other, the silent gobbler retreated in defeat with the jake. The excited gobbler had won, and he chased and gobbled after the interlopers, seeming to forget about his prize. Like flies on a wall, we had witnessed some spectacular yet seldom seen turkey behavior.

Seeing the gobblers departing from the stage before us, I came up with an idea. I whispered to the shaking, camouflaged blob on my right to take off his baseball cap, and to whack it intermittently against his knee to sound like the fighting birds' wings hitting each other. Quickly pulling out my Knight & Hale Fighting Purr calls, I imitated the alternating, aggressive purring we had just heard.

Seconds after starting our mock fight, the victorious gobbler was running straight toward us with wings down and feathers bristled in an aggressive posture. He nearly ran right over us in our shaking boots! All of us thought the bruiser was going to flail us, just like he had done to his vanquished foe.

Momentarily the tom zigzagged in front of us too close for my telephoto lens to focus but long enough to leave an image that will replay in my mind for the rest of my life.

Shopping for New Hunting Binoculars

BY BOB ROBB

When shopping for new binoculars or a new spotting scope, remember only one word: quality. Buying the best binoculars you can afford is a lifetime investment in increased hunting success. I've never heard a discouraging word from hunters who carry binoculars from Zeiss, Swarovski, Bausch & Lomb or Leica, which also happen to be the most expensive. Simmons, Nikon, Burris, Fujinon, Pentax, Leupold and Steiner also make good binoculars that cost less money.

Advanced big game hunters also know that even though they weigh more, full-sized binoculars with relatively large objective lenses are easier to hold steady, and their larger lenses allow them to see better in dim dawn and dusk light, when game is most active. That's why they avoid compact binoculars.

Unless you shop at a camera store or serious hunting shop with an experienced staff, you'll get little help when trying to select a new pair of binoculars. The best way is to compare as many brands as possible side by side outside the store.

"Shop at a store with a good selection so you can make valid comparisons," advises Barbara Mellman, head of public relations for Bushnell and Bausch & Lomb binoculars for more than 20 years. "Call the dealer up and tell them you're seriously shopping, and ask if you can come over and test several binoculars outside in a 'real world' environment. Shopping at sunset is the best time, or on a cloudy or rainy day, so you can compare in dim light."

Take several different makes and models to a shaded area, and sit down. It's best not to look over pavement, because heat distortion can be a problem. Looking over grass is better. Choose a distant object to focus on, like a tree limb outlined against the sky 100 yards away. Does it appear crisp and sharp, or is it soft? Next, spend a little time looking around, concentrating on small, complex shapes at various distances. My favorite test is to look into dark, shaded areas. If I can't see into them well, I'm not happy.

Just as important, when you take the binoculars away from your eyes, can you see perfectly without the feeling that your eyes are trying hard to refocus themselves? If so, there might be a problem with the binoculars' collimation. One of the most difficult tasks in binocular manufacturing is perfectly aligning both lenses so that you are looking in exactly the same direction with both eyes. Using binoculars with faulty collimation leads to severe eyestrain.

"Select different brands of the power and objective lens size you have decided on," Mellman suggests. "Then find out how comfortably they fit in your hand. Outside, look into dark areas or corners to get a feeling for the relative brightness of each. Then weigh in other factors, including brightness, clarity, comfort, exterior comfort of holding and carrying them, waterproofness and the manufacturer's reputation and warranty program. The last thing you should consider, though, is price. When buying binoculars, you really do get what you pay for."

Understanding Binocular Numbers

Binoculars are identified by a simple code; simple, that is, if you understand the code. This is how Bushnell Sports Optics Worldwide explains the binocular numbering system.

The code is usually two numbers separated by an "X," for example, 7X35. The first number is the power or magnification of the binoculars. With 7X35 binoculars, the object being viewed appears to 7 times closer than you would see it with the unaided eye.

The exit pupil is the column of light that comes through the binoculars. The larger the exit pupil, the brighter the image will be in lower light conditions. To determine the size of the exit pupil, divide the second number by the first (for example, with the 7X35, 35 divided by 7 equals 5). Using your binoculars in low light conditions, an exit pupil diameter of 5mm or greater is best. For normal circumstances, 3 to 5mm works well.

The second number in the performance formula (7X35) is the diameter of the objective, that is, the front lens, in millimeters. The larger the objective lens, the more light can enter the binoculars, and the brighter the image will be.

—Glenn Sapir

PRONGHORN

NAME:
George Abbot

RESIDENCE:
Canton, NC

WHERE TAKEN:
Laramie, Wyoming

ARMS USED:
.300 Winchester Mag Rifle

George was hunting with Southern Wyoming Outfitters.

Decisions to Make Before Contacting Outfitters

- What animal do I want to hunt, and by which method do I prefer to hunt?

- How important is it that I harvest an animal? Am I willing to pass up legal animals for a remote chance at a record-book animal?

- How much am I willing to spend? Remember to include airfare, taxidermy fees, license costs, guide fees and tip.

- How important is the type of country? Is it mandatory that the hunt be in the mountains? Or would I be happy hunting the edge of an alfalfa field? Be honest.

- How important are the accommodations? Is staying in an outfitter's wall tent far away from civilization required? Would I be happy staying in a hotel on the edge of town and driving to the hunting area each day?

—Dan Dietrich

Bobwhite Quail

COLINUS VIRGINIANUS

OTHER NAMES:

Bob, bobwhite, quail

CHARACTERISTICS:

Quail of brushlands, fields and edges: Cocks and hens are mottled brown, with lighter undersides and a gray tail. The male's face is black and white, the female's is buff and brown. A full-grown bird will only weigh 6 to 8 ounces!

HABITAT:

Bobwhites love a lazy farmer, whose place has abandoned fields, a couple of woodlots, brushy edges or overgrown fencerows, maybe an active grainfield or two. Like so many gamebirds, "edge" cover is key.

FOOD:

Seeds of all kinds, along with grasses and other small leaves. When available, small grains are important, as are acorns, berries and insects in season.

BEHAVIOR:

Homebodies. Bobwhites will make their daily travels within one small area—feeding in early morning, loafing in brushy cover during the day, heading back out to open areas to feed in the late afternoon, then roosting in thick cover at night. The birds will live in coveys of 12 to 18 birds. If flushed and separated, they will call to each other with their telltale "bob-white" and "hoo-hee-hoo" whistles, until they are all gathered again.

NESTING:

After attracting a mate with his "bob-white" calls, a cock will scratch out a shallow nest in the grass or brush. He will stay with the hen after she lays their 12 to16 eggs, and even help raise the brood … a true gentleman of the gamebird world!

HUNTING STRAGETIES:

Pointing dogs are the classic way to hunt quail. Cover a lot of country, and be ready for the whirring flush of a whole bunch of birds. Pick one out and if you hit it, mark the spot well. Treat a covey of quail with respect and restraint—they are a delicate resource that should be hunted only lightly and with care so that enough birds will persist until next year.   —Tom Carpenter

TIPS AFIELD

Keeping Optics Clean Afield

It's a never ending struggle that plagues hunters every time they set foot outside: how to keep binoculars and rifle scope lenses clean while out in the field. Dust, pollen, mildew and other airborne particles that settle on the lens can lead to buildup and cause impairment in the visual quality of your optics.

The first barrier in the line of defense, according to Carl Zeiss Optical, Inc., is always to store the equipment with the lens cap on. It is also recommended that you keep the lens caps on until putting the binoculars or scope to use.

If you see dirt or fingerprints on the lens, blow on the lens. This will remove loose debris. If that doesn't remove all of the dirt, rub a soft cloth in a circular motion over the area. A cotton ball or commercial lens cleaning cloth will provide the best results. *Do not use paper tissue*; it can scratch the coating of the lens. Excessive cleaning can actually lead to scratching, which harms the lens more than the dust. These scratches cause the light to scatter when entering the optical instrument, decreasing its performance. If the lens gets scratched, contact the manufacturer. Repair can be a lot cheaper than replacement.

Rifle Cleaning Musts

1. Always clean a rifle as soon as possible after using it. The longer you leave the barrel dirty, the higher the potential for corrosion damaging the bore.

2. Use modern solvents that remove copper and powder fouling and keep cleaning until you have patches coming out white, indicating all fouling has been removed.

3. Always clean from the breech, if possible, using a bore guide. If you must clean from the muzzle, use a rod guide to protect the crown from damage.

4. Before storing a rifle for any length of time or after cleaning, always use a protectant on the bore and other exposed metal surfaces to prevent rust.

5. Before firing, always wipe the bore clean with a patch or two to remove any excessive residual oil.

6. Fire a fouling shot before hunting. Some rifles will shoot to a different point of aim with a clean bore than they will from a fouled bore. This is particularly true when there are traces of oil or other protectants in the bore. —Bryce Towsley

Recipes

Back Forty Roast

Ingredients

2 to 4 lbs. venison or moose roast
3 cloves garlic, peeled
6 wild onion bulbs peeled—
  yard variety, found
  everywhere
1/4 cup pepper vinegar
1 tbsp. Lea & Perrins Sauce

1 tbsp. crushed rosemary
1/2 tsp. crushed thyme
1/2 tsp. crushed basil
1/2 stick margarine or butter
  sprinkle of ground red pepper
1/2 cup wine (I prefer white
  Rhine)

Preparation

Marinate spices and liquids until softened. Trim roast and pat dry. With paring knife, puncture holes in roast and push in clove and onion bulbs. Place roast on heavy-duty aluminum foil and place in cast iron skillet. Sprinkle lightly with ground red pepper. Pour marinade over roast, put margarine or butter on top and fold foil over the top. Put into 350°F preheated oven. (One hour for two pounds and under, one and one half hours for over two pounds.) After allotted time, turn oven off and let cool in oven overnight. Make gravy from drippings and serve over meat or potatoes.

Rudy Goodrich
Yorktown, VA

Mountain Lion

FELIS CONCOLOR

OTHER NAMES:

Puma, cougar, panther, catamount

CHARACTERISTICS:

Coat gray to yellowish- or reddish-brown; colors usually deepest along back with whitish shades on underside; head small and rounded with very short face; eyes set forward on head for sight hunting; ears short and rounded; body long and lithe; tail long, round, black-tipped; adult males weigh 150 to 190 lbs., females 70 to 120 pounds.

HABITAT:

Mostly mountains and foothills, but any habitat with sufficient food, cover and room to avoid humans.

FOOD:

Deer, elk and porcupines are most important, but take prey ranging in size from grasshoppers to moose.

BEHAVIOR:

Solitary, except for females accompanied by males or kittens. Females den in caves, rock crevices, brush piles, etc., with kittens and leave them while hunting; usually hunt by stealth at night and cover unused food for later use; males territorial, and large male home ranges may overlap smaller ones of females.

REPRODUCTION:

Breed any time, but young most commonly born in May; two to four spotted young born about every 2 years per female; females keep males away from kittens, who may otherwise eat them; females first breed at 2 to 4 years of age.

HUNTING:

Where it's legal, it's done with dogs on long chases through some awfully rough country.

Hunter's Log

*t*his hunter's log will make it simple for you to capture hunting memories and record the important details of your hunts. Make copies of this page and fill it in for every hunt you go on.

Date:_____   Hunting tools used: _____

Base camp: _____   Shots taken:_____

Location hunted:_____   Time: _____

_____   Distance: _____

Type of terrain: _____   Misses:_____

Companions: _____   Hits: _____

_____   Wildlife seen (species, number, time, location, what they were

Weather: _____   doing):_____

Time hunt began: _____   _____

Time hunt ended: _____   _____

Game harvested (species, number, physical statistics—weight, length, antler/horn specs): _____

_____

_____

Companions' experiences: _____

_____

_____

Other noteworthy aspects of the hunt: _____

_____

_____

After Your Elk Is Down

When your bull elk is down and found, you have achieved elk hunting success, but your job is not over, says Brad Harris, Team Realtree member.

"Now you are working against the clock, temperature and other conditions to preserve the prime meat," Harris explains.

"Considering elk size, on-the-spot butchering is the most common option. The goal is two-fold: You want to get the carcass cooled quickly and to get it cut up into manageable chunks for easy transport. Some skin the elk immediately, because warm skin comes off easier. They then use the skin, flesh side up, as a clean surface on which to lay chunks of meat. Others gut and quarter with the skin left on to protect the meat, in its natural wrapper, during transport."

"Either way, quick cooling is essential for top meat quality. In the West, a shady spot offers cool air and breezes even on a warm day. Get the meat out of the sun and protect it from insects with meat bags. Then begin packing it out."

Understanding Bloat Can Save Your Dog's Life

Bloat, or gastric dilatation, is not a dietary disease. This disorder of the digestive system has been poorly understood, according to Dr. Dottie Laflamme, a veterinary nutritionist for Ralston Purina.

Bloat is characterized by expansion of the stomach with gas or frothy material (dilatation). The stomach will not empty normally; it is difficult for food to advance into the intestines, and it will not pass in the other direction as vomit.

Dilatation can be followed by a rotation of the stomach, called volvulus, which closes both entry to and exit from the stomach, so that relief of the distended state is not possible. This rotation compresses one of the major veins carrying blood to the heart, severely depressing normal blood circulation. This can quickly lead to shock and death.

Bloat primarily affects deep-chested, mature members of large breeds, but it also has been reported in small dogs. More cases are reported in April and August, when dogs are likely more active.

Purina experts suggest some steps to decrease the chances of bloat:

- Do not allow your dog to become overweight.

- Feed several small meals throughout the day instead of one large meal.

- If you have more than one dog, feed the dogs individually in a quiet place to help calm eager eaters who may swallow a lot of air when eating.

- Do not feed your dog immediately before or after vigorous exercise.

- Sudden diet changes can trigger gastric upsets. Change a dog's diet gradually over a period of 7 to 10 days. Begin with a small amount of the new food and gradually increase this amount each day.

- Be alert to symptoms such as abdominal swelling and unproductive vomiting.

- Consult your regular veterinarian if you suspect problems.

Care for Your Aging Hunting Dog

All dogs, at any age, deserve the utmost care you can provide. Mature dogs, however, may require special attention. Here are some tips from Ralston Purina concerning care for the aging hunting dog.

- Dogs are creatures of habit. Any drastic alteration in the dog's daily routine should be kept to a minimum.
- Keep your dog's bed in a dry and draft-free area. Older dogs feel the effects of extremes of heat and cold more than younger ones. Make sure the dog is thoroughly dried after a bath, rain or snow. In hot, humid weather, keep the older dog in air conditioning.
- Older dogs may tend to groom themselves less. Regular grooming helps remove the dead hair and is an excellent time to inspect for external parasites or skin disorders.
- Moderate exercise helps to maintain circulation and stimulates muscle tone. On hunting trips, if you are taking your own vehicle and have room, take your older dog along for moderate, gentle exercise before hunting.
- A gradual decline in kidney function is not unusual. The older dog may tend to have more accidents, especially at night, or want to go out more frequently.

- Always keep clean, fresh water readily available. In winter, use a heated bowl to keep water from freezing.
- Keeping the physical environment of the dog's surroundings the same will help the dog to adjust to reduced capability and failing eyesight. Some dogs may also suffer some loss of smell.
- Don't be too overly anxious to introduce a pup to the older dog's environment. This might accelerate the older dog's degeneration as he receives less attention.
- An annual physical examination by the veteranarian is a must. Your vet may advise more frequent examinations to more closely monitor the dog's condition.
- As the dog's activity declines, the food intake may need to be adjusted to help prevent obesity. Obesity can make a dog more susceptible to problems with an impaired heart, breathing and liver functions, digestive disturbances and increased stress on the skeleton, ligaments, joints and tendons, which, in turn, can lead to degenerative arthritis.

Overcalling Elk

Elk calling is a dramatic way to hunt elk. It has all the appeal of turkey calling, but the game you call in is far bigger than a gobbler.

The bugle is the loudest and most dramatic elk call, according to Brad Harris, expert hunter and member of Team Realtree.

"The high-pitched, keening whistle of a mature bull has real ear appeal, whether it is made by you or, even better, by a big bull in the black timber, answering you," Harris said.

"However, bugling can be overdone and often is. Many hunters bugle all the time, and the bulls get both tired and wary of it. Also, it can drive subdominant bulls away and cause harem bosses to take their cows and leave.

"Cow calling is far more subtle and subdued.

The mews and chirps made by cow elk (bulls make these same sounds much less frequently) are 'confidence calls' that assure all is well. Most elk, including bulls, will investigate cow calls, even after the bugling season is over."

Brad Harris

Recipes

Kyle's Smothered Dove

Ingredients

6   doves
1/2 cup margarine
1   small bunch of
    green onions, chopped

1/8 tsp. pepper
1/2 tsp. salt
1 1/2 cups water

Preparation

Cook onions in margarine on low heat until slightly yellow. Rub doves with salt and pepper, then sauté doves in mixture until well-browned. Add water, cover and simmer 45 minutes.

Dove in a Blanket

Ingredients

2 dove breasts per person
salt and pepper

2 strips bacon

Preparation

Rub dove breasts with salt and pepper. Wrap each with a strip of bacon. Fold each piece in aluminum foil. Place in baking dish and bake electrically at 300°F for 2 hours. Serve hot with buttered, steamed wild rice.

Kyle Streit
Electra, TX

CARIBOU

HUNTER:
Michael J. Sexton

RESIDENCE:
Wyandotte, MI

WHERE TAKEN:
Quebec, Canada

ARMS USED:
Remington .300 Mag Rifle

Michael was hunting with Canadadventure.

HUNTERS:
Linda & Ron Neifert

RESIDENCE:
Wichita, KS

WHERE TAKEN:
Northwest Territories, Canada

ARMS USED:
Linda used a Remington 700 .270 Winchester Mountain Rifle; Ron used Winchester Model 70 Super Grade .270 Winchester Rifle.

The Neiferts pulled off a double when they hunted barren ground caribou with Barry Taylor of Arctic Safaris. Linda poses with her bull; life member Ron, along with Linda, stands over his prize.

BEARS

NAME:
Tom Garvin

RESIDENCE:
Rising Sun, MD

WHERE TAKEN:
Alaska

ARMS USED:
Ruger 77 .338 Mag Rifle

Tom got this giant brown bear with the assistance of guide Robert Hardy of Bucking Horse Ranch.

NAME:
Terry K. Miller

RESIDENCE:
Benezett, PA

WHERE TAKEN:
Vancouver Island,
British Columbia,
Canada

ARMS USED:
.30-06 Rifle; 180-Grain
Sierra SPBT

Terry, guided by Clay Lancaster of NWT Outfitters Ltd., got this big bruin.

Hunting Humor

Tomasic art

Early Scouting Pays Off

Alate-summer look at your deer hunting area can pay dividends come opening day. Of course, for bowhunters, these benefits are pretty direct. Late summer blends easily into early fall, and most deer patterns change little before the opening of early bow seasons.

That's some basic advice from Brenda Valentine, professional outdoor writer and seminar speaker on woodscraft, wildlife and hunting.

"However, there is a slight and subtle shift of feeding patterns," she continues. "Grasses and forbs are beginning to dry out and deer are seeking juicier morsels. Cornfields are good bets as the ears ripen, and apple orchards are becoming very attractive. Both of these will remain good bets into the fall," Valentine advises.

"Wild fruits rather than buds are becoming available. Persimmons, wild crabapples, hawthorns and a variety of other fall fruits and berries are

ripening now, and deer seem to know these things won't last. They feed heavily on fall fruits while they are available."

"Bowhunters should take note of what deer-favored fall fruits are available in their area and are becoming available during the bow season. Before the rut, hunting a food source is a good bet," Valentine says.

Summer Care for Your Gun Dog

When temperatures soar, hunters should remember that summer can be extremely hard on their four-legged partners, reminds the Louisiana Department of Wildlife and Fisheries.

- Many veterinarians agree that providing fresh water is probably the most important requirement in caring for a dog during the summer. Dogs should be given fresh water at least once a day. On extremely hot days, dogs will require a lot of water.

- Sporting dogs that are overlooked during summer's heat usually aren't ready to hunt when fall rolls around. Dog owners who dedicate a little time each day to their canines will be pleased with the hunting performance of their dogs on opening day. A healthy, active dog can make all the difference in a hunting experience.

- Sun is a dog's mortal enemy, especially for dark-colored breeds like black labs. A tree or two in the backyard can make a big difference. In a yard without trees, build a simple cover using four posts and a piece of plywood. Position it so a breeze blows beneath it.

- While these precautions help keep a dog comfortable through the summer, sporting dogs still won't be ready for opening day without adequate exercise. Dogs need to run for about 30 minutes daily. Schedule exercise periods for the dog in early morning or late evening to avoid heat stroke.

- Control of external and internal parasites also helps dogs remain healthy and comfortable in the summertime. Bathe dogs regularly with a quality flea or tick shampoo. Dips also do a good job of solving these summer pest problems.

- Internal parasites can keep a dog in a rundown condition during the summer and on into the fall hunting season. This problem can be solved easily by the veterinarian.

- Spend some time on your sport dog in the summer, and he will come through for you in the fall.

Hard Hunting; Easy Cleaning

BY JOEL YOUNG

The third weekend of October in Minnesota always offers four wonderfully long ruffed grouse hunting days over the weekend of the state teacher convention. Since my father and I are both teachers and avid grouse hunters, we take every advantage that those four days offer to hunt.

We regularly hunt in the same locations each fall and can count on bagging at least a brace of grouse on any given day—even when the grouse are at the bottom of their cycle. In good years we can count on bagging close to our limit (a decent feat when you consider the fact that we don't hunt over dogs).

As I made the typically long walk down one of my favorite trails, I felt a sudden urge to stop walking and look to my right. Normally I hunt at a moderately slow pace and stop occasionally to try to spook birds into flushing. But this time I was pulled to a stop by an unintentional internal force. I had half-turned to my right when I heard the faint cluck of a grouse. "Stupid grouse," I thought to myself. I quickly scanned the ground to locate it. Nothing. Not a trace.

The next thought to run through my head was an expletive about how well that "stupid grouse" was camouflaged. It never ceases to amaze me how completely invisible they can be on the ground, even when they are a foot or two in front of you.

In a sudden explosion, the grouse flushed vertically from its hiding spot less than 15 feet from me. Unfortunately for the grouse, the cover it was in was a bit too thick to make a speedy escape. About 10 feet off the ground its wings starting hitting the twigs and branches of the young poplar, slowing it down just long enough for me to get my stunned brain in gear. Just as the grouse cleared the top of the saplings, its wings folded up and it dropped back to earth like a stone. A clean kill, or so I believed.

After marking the spot it had fallen, I quickly recovered the limp, lifeless body and stuffed it into my vest. Feeling good about the success of a somewhat lucky snap shot, I continued on down the trail. I walked another couple hundred yards to the end of the trail and turned around. All in all I thought that the trail had been unusually uneventful. I had only flushed one bird on the trail, when typically I would flush at least four. When I came upon the spot where I had bagged the grouse earlier, that same thought ran through my head, "stupid grouse, if you had only kept quiet you wouldn't be lying dead in the game pouch of my vest." I had continued walking back toward the truck for about another 15 or so minutes when I almost jumped out of my boots.

A tremendously violent fluttering was going on in the game pouch of my vest. I couldn't believe what was happening. The grouse that I had shot dead more than 40 minutes ago was suddenly alive and thrashing about in my vest! Before I could react, the grouse propelled itself out the back opening of the vest like a bullet. I now had an "undead" grouse running frantically down the trail dragging a broken wing. It actually turned its head back toward me as it was running away as if to say, "I'm not so stupid after all, am I?"

My first thought was to run after this crazed bird, but then I realized that I could end up chasing it over hill and dale

without success. I stopped, let it run a few more yards down the trail, leveled my shotgun and ended the lunacy once and for all. As the feathers settled, I retrieved the grouse again, thinking that I had unfortunately mutilated the bird to no end. On the ground was a streak of feathers and a newly exposed 5-foot long strip of dirt on the trail. The blast had hit the grouse in the butt and had taken out the tail, spine, guts, head and all. I held in my hand a feathered breast with two wings—nothing more, and not a single pellet in the breast. Finally, this crafty grouse had met its end. And I had saved myself some cleaning duty.

GETTING READY

How to Transport Your Hunting Dog

It's sad that many dogs are lost each year while traveling, says Bob West, well-known dog trainer and a consultant for Ralston Purina. Common causes, he explains, include overheating in closed vehicles and carbon monoxide poisoning from exhaust leaks in pickup campers. Even the best equipment, through misuse or lack of concern or understanding, can cost your dog's life.

Your dog must be confined while traveling. A loose dog in a moving vehicle is unsafe no matter how well-trained. The least he might do is eat your lunch and, at worst, he could cause a traffic accident. Forget about letting him loose in the back of a pickup.

Shade and ventilation are your primary concerns. The temperature inside a closed station wagon in direct sunlight can climb to over 100°F even though the outside temperature may be in the 40s.

Here's a traveling checklist:

❏ Check ventilation.

❏ Avoid direct sunlight on unattended vehicles.

❏ Tie down slide-in kennels while traveling.

❏ Familiarize your dogs with kennels before the trip.

❏ Wet dogs will heat up in closed compartments.

❏ Stop every hour for a potty break.

❏ Offer small amounts of water during stops.

❏ Don't feed or water too much before or during travel.

❏ Good clean bedding adds comfort and warmth during cold weather.

❏ Be certain exhaust gases aren't present.

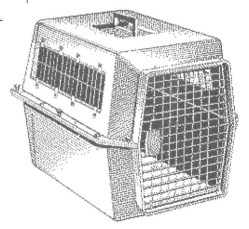

Hit Where It Counts

J oe Drake is a top game caller and hunter, having won more than 20 game calling titles. He is an avid deer hunter and offers advice about where he likes to place his shots:

"My preferred aiming points on deer depend on whether I'm hunting with a bow or a gun. With a bow, it's an easy call. I shoot for the chest area behind the shoulder. Straight-down shots into the spine worry me. Today's powerful bows and strong broadheads can make this shot into the spine or through the three inches or so of loin muscle. But when I can, I avoid bone, including shoulder bones, with bows."

"With rifles it's a very different deal,"

the Team Realtree member points out. "I actually aim for bone to maximize expanding bullet performance, produce more shock and get a quicker kill. Square on the shoulder is hard to beat. If I'm in a rock-solid stand, particularly with a shooting rail, and the deer presents the right shot, I'll go for the neck."

"I don't like head shots because a slight miss is a major wound on a deer that I am unlikely to recover. Spine shots mess up the best meat, and rear-end shots can go wrong too easily," Drake warns.

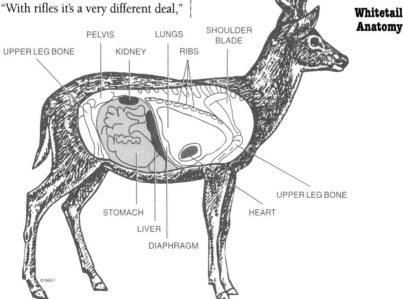

Whitetail Anatomy

UPPER LEG BONE · PELVIS · KIDNEY · LUNGS · RIBS · SHOULDER BLADE

STOMACH · LIVER · DIAPHRAGM · HEART · UPPER LEG BONE

©NBEF

Pack It Up

BY DAN DIETRICH

Before you put an end to the hunting season, take care of these 10 important tasks. Then, you'll be ready for the next opener.

1 **Make a Gear Wish List.** While the hunting season is fresh in your mind, make note of gear you need for a more comfortable, productive season next time around.

2 **Protect Your Firearms.** Clean your firearms. Apply a thin coat of oil or silicone. If your gun jammed or gave you problems, now is the time to take it to the gunsmith. Finally, make sure all guns are safely stored. It's the perfect time to look for a gun safe; stores reduce prices on hunting supplies after the season.

3 **Record Important Hunting Data & Save Informative Magazine Articles.** Over time, the seasons and their details start to blur together. Record hunting data onto a topo map or plastic overlay. It helps remind you of where the game was.

Create folders labeled by subject and file favorite magazine articles for future reference.

4 **Keep Your Boots in Good Shape.** Follow the boot care instructions that came with your boots. On full-grain or oil-tanned leather boots, clean off dirt and grime with a damp cloth. Remove stubborn dirt with a soft brush. Allow boots to dry at room temperature. Then apply a leather dressing, such as mink oil to protect the leather and keep it from drying out.

If your boots are injected with silicone to make them waterproof, do not use a leather dressing. Instead, clean the boots as described above and let them dry. Then apply a light coat of silicone.

Cordura boots simply need to be cleaned with a damp cloth and allowed to dry at room temperature.

Rubber boots, including hip-boots and waders, should be cleaned with soap and water. The rubber can be protected with a rubber conditioner. Store them in a cool, dry place.

5 **Clean Hunting Optics.** For general cleaning, dust off lens surfaces with a soft camera brush. For more thorough cleaning, lubricate the lens by breathing on it or by applying an eyeglass lens cleaner. Then use a soft cloth to slowly wipe the lens clean in a circular motion. Use a cotton-tipped swab to gently remove dirt and grime from the outside edge of the lens. Also, do not polish the lens, and take care not to scratch the thin, colored coating on the lens surface.

6 **Repair & Improve Other Hunting Equipment.** Now is the best time to clean, fix and maintain the other equipment you used during the season.

❏ Put a new edge on your hunting knife.

❏ Lubricate a noisy bolt on your treestand.

❏ Seam seal your rain gear.

❏ Update your survival kit.

7 **Maintain Good Landowner Relations.** Take time to talk to the landowner. Ask if there were any problems during the season. Find out if there is anything he would like you to do differently next year. For gaining permission on new lands, use the quiet season of winter as the time to approach prospective property owners.

8 **Take Inventory.** Sort through the freezer to see what game you have, and rearrange the meat so the oldest is in the front. On an upright freezer, store all the meat from one year on one shelf, the meat from the previous season on another.

9 **Record Upcoming Application Deadline.** Many applications for the next season are due in early spring. Take the time now to mark the appropriate deadlines on your calendar.

10 **Help Protect Our Hunting Heritage.** Do something to help protect and promote our hunting tradition. Join a wildlife conservation group, for example. Or help at the grassroots level. Volunteer for projects with local groups. Spend time with your son or daughter, just hiking through the woods and enjoying the outdoors. Expand the number of hunting opportunities available to you. Try bowhunting or muzzleloading if they are new to you. Help a friend get started.

Lemon Barbecued Rabbit

Ingredients

1 rabbit, cut into serving
   pieces
3/4 cup and 2 tsp. flour
2 tsp. salt
1/4 tsp. pepper

1/3 cup butter
1 tsp. kitchen bouquet
2 tbs. sugar

LEMON SAUCE
1 clove garlic
2 1/2 tsp. salt
1/3 cup salad oil
1/2 cup lemon juice

3/4 cup water
1/4 cup finely chopped onion
1 tsp. black pepper
1 tsp. ground thyme

Preparation

Prepare Lemon Sauce: Crush garlic with salt. Add salad oil, lemon juice, water, onion, pepper and thyme. Mix well and let sit overnight.

Marinate rabbit in Lemon Sauce for 2 hours. Remove rabbit and dry it slightly. Combine 3/4 cup flour, salt and pepper. Roll rabbit in flour mixture. Brown well in butter. Combine lemon sauce and kitchen bouquet; pour over rabbit and cover. Cook over low heat for 45 minutes or until rabbit is tender. Remove rabbit and place on hot platter. Combine 2 tsp. flour, cold water and sugar to sauce. Heat and stir to boiling. Serve over rabbit. 4 servings.

Daniel Cosby
Appling, GA

Ruffed Grouse

BONASA UMBELLUS

OTHER NAMES:

Grouse, ruff, partridge, pat, chicken

CHARACTERISTICS:

A gamebird of woodlands and thickets, a grouse's most prominent feature is the rounded, fanned tail. Two color phases dominate—red or gray—but almost innumerable variations and combinations exist among grouse. No two birds are exactly alike! A beautiful "ruff" of feathers surrounds the neck on cocks. The best way to tell cocks from hens when you have a bird in hand: a cock's dark-colored tailband is unbroken. An adult grouse of either sex will weigh 1 to 1^1/2 pounds.

HABITAT:

Ruffed grouse are birds of young forest and thick brush. They like this cover around them and need the overhead protection the branches, vines and leaves provide ... but they do not usually like much grassy cover. Mixed woodlands with aspen, and plenty of edges between big and small timber, timber and wetlands or timber and other openings should exist. These edges are the spots where grouse will hang out.

FOOD:

Buds, fruits and catkins from trees and shrubs. Berries and other small fruits. Seeds and green leaves, such as clover, picked off the forest floor.

BEHAVIOR:

A grouse is a homebody and, once he or she finds a suitable piece of habitat, might not stray from a 40-acre area again.

NESTING:

In early spring, a cock will find a log atop which he will strut, fan his tail and drum, in an attempt to attract a hen. She will find a very dense thicket to nest in, building a small depression at the base of a tree, laying 8 to 14 buff-colored eggs.

HUNTING STRAGETIES:

You can hunt grouse effectively without a dog if you stop-go-stop-go as you work through good cover. Stick to the "edges" mentioned. A good, close-ranging dog can help, but he or she must be under control and stay close, otherwise you'll never get a shot. Always be ready for the thunderous flush!

—Tom Carpenter

TIPS AFIELD

Elk Pointers

When you bowhunt for elk, you are magnifying your archery challenge. Obviously elk are bigger and tougher than deer. Unlike gun hunters, bowhunters can't simply step up to a more powerful magnum weapon. In order to maximize trajectory, range and penetration, most archers are already shooting as much bow as they can handle for deer. That's fine.

Those are the sentiments of world-famous bowhunter Chuck Adams, a member of Team Realtree.

"Arrows kill by hemorrhage, not by shock. If your bow can put a razor-sharp broadhead deep into an elk's heart/lung area, it will bag the bull," Adams warns.

"The point is the point. Elk hunting broadheads should be strong, tough and top quality. The edges must be razor sharp. The point should be designed for maximum penetration. Two-blade broadheads penetrate efficiently, but three-blade designs do almost as well and offer more total cutting surface. Wide heads offer even more width of cut but sacrifice considerable penetration."

"With good, sharp, high-penetration broadheads," Adams concludes, "you will be able to shoot through a broadside elk with a reasonably powerful 'deer-class' bow."

MUSKOX

NAME:
Pete Studwell

RESIDENCE:
Port Chester, NY

WHERE TAKEN:
Northwest Territories,
Canada

ARMS USED:
7mm Mag. Remington
Rifle

Pete was hunting with Charlie Ruben Outfitters, based in Univik, NWT, when he got his muskox.

NAME:
Fred Felbab

RESIDENCE:
Berlin, WI

WHERE TAKEN:
Banks Island,
Northwest Territories,
Canada

ARMS USED:
Recurve Bow; Cedar
Arrows, Tipped With
Bear Razorheads

Fred set out with guide Frank Kudlak of the Banks Island Hunter/Trapper Assn. when he arrowed this muskox.

R E C I P E S

Recipes

Quick Venison & Rice Platter

Ingredients

1½ to 2 lbs. ground venison
3 tbs. margarine or butter
  (oil if you prefer)
1¾ cups beef bouillon
  (may use 6 bouillon cubes
  or instant bouillon with
  warm water)
3 tbs. ketchup
¼ tsp. salt

1 medium to large onion,
  chopped
3 tbs. flour
⅓ cup cold water
1 cup dairy sour cream
2 cups cooked rice
1 (10-oz.) can sliced
  mushrooms, optional

Preparation

In a 10-inch or larger skillet, cook and stir ground venison in margarine until brown. Stir bouillon, ketchup, garlic, salt and onion into skillet. Heat to boiling, reduce heat. Cover and simmer for 5 minutes.

Shake flour and cold water in tightly covered container; stir gradually into venison mixture. Optional mushrooms should be added at this time. Heat to boiling, stirring constantly. Boil and stir for 1 minute; reduce heat. Stir in sour cream; heat through.

Serve over prepared rice or stir prepared rice into mixture for fast and easy serving. Serve with your favorite vegetable and bread for a delicious yet quick meal.

Duane E. Jones
Parkersburg, WV

TIPS AFIELD

5 Keys to Archery Accuracy
BY CHUCK ADAMS

Pinpoint paper-punching is an essential first step toward bowhunting accuracy, nailing a breathing buck is more complex than hitting a bull's-eye. Graduate from range shooting to natural objects in realistic field situations. This is called stump shooting. This still falls short of shooting at big game, which requires sound judgment and steady nerves. Nothing short of hunting experience can teach you control. You can help prepare for the test, however, by memorizing these five crucial steps:

1 **Be Ready to Shoot.** Make certain your armguard, bowstring release aid, fanny pack and other items are in proper place. If you climb into a treestand, attach your safety belt, hang your bow within easy reach, take rangefinder readings and prepare for an immediate shot. Avoid physical discomfort by wearing proper clothing.

2 **Shoot at the Right Time.** Never shoot at a suspicious or fully alert animal. Never draw if you can see an animal's eye. Animal body angle must be correct to ensure a quickly lethal hit. Rear-quartering shots expose the entire chest cavity.

3 **Don't Dillydally Your Shot.** When the shooting time is right, you must release then or forever hold your peace. Expert bowhunters take the first reasonable shot that is offered.

4 **Aim Precisely at the Vitals.** It is your responsibility as a bowhunter to understand animal anatomy. To harvest game consistently, you must aim deliberately at the center of the vitals. As an animal approaches, rivet your eyes on the vital zone, pick out a tiny aiming spot and ignore the rest of the animal.

5 **Follow Through.** You must concentrate on your target, hold your bow and continue to aim until the arrow strikes. It is easy to anticipate, drop your bow and lift your head; this destroys accurate shooting form and causes arrows to hit off center.

Mountain Goat

OREAMNOS AMERICANUS

OTHER NAMES:

Rocky Mountain goat

CHARACTERISTICS:

Coat white, horns and hooves black; tail may have a few black or brown hairs; long hair of winter coat forms a beard under the chin and pantaloons around the front legs; body compact and chunky, legs short; horns smooth, sharp and curve slightly backward, 8 to 10 inches long; horns of nannies curve less and are thinner, but sometimes longer than those of billies; hooves have hard outer edges with soft centers that "stick" to rocks; old billies may weigh 300 pounds or more, nannies about 150 pounds.

HABITAT:

Precipitous terrain; steep, south-facing slopes in winter; sometimes enter subalpine forests.

FOOD:

Grasses, sedges, lichens, forbs and shrubs.

BEHAVIOR:

Nannies, kids and immature billies form small herds; mature billies are often alone except during rut; females dominant over males.

REPRODUCTION:

Breed in November and December; usually one kid, but sometimes two on good range; billies fight head to tail, sometimes inflicting serious wounds to hindquarters and flanks. Nannies usually breed at 2$\frac{1}{2}$ years of age.

HUNTING:

Get in shape and get up high. Glass, glass, glass and then stalk carefully—goats are not geniuses but they will not sit around if you kick a few rocks or ignore the wind.

Learning Turkey Talk

oday's advanced turkey call designs make good calling technique much easier to master than it used to be, but going in cold is not the way to go gobbler hunting. A bit of preseason practice helps any turkey caller, and it is vital if you are trying to master a new call type.

Those are the thoughts of Will Primos, well-known call manufacturer and turkey hunter.

"The many turkey hunting videos available are a good and enjoyable way to learn what turkeys sound like," Primos recommends. "As you watch them also watch how the live turkeys respond to calling. This great learning tool has become available only in the last few years. The purely instructional videos and audio tapes go into great detail. My call company makes these, and so do many others."

"Also look at the 'novice friendly' call types that are available. These and some designed especially for young people are great ways to learn to use a new call type. Just remember," Primos advises, "any new endeavor takes a little practice before you become proficient."

Will Primos

BEARS

SOMETHING TO SHOOT FOR

NAME:
John Giammarco

RESIDENCE:
Hinsdale, NH

WHERE TAKEN:
Maine

ARMS USED:
Sako .300 Winchester
Mag Rifle

John with his Maine black bear.

NAME:
Dale Brewster

RESIDENCE:
Stanley, ND

WHERE TAKEN:
Fairview, Alberta

Dale took both of these bruins with Doig River Outfitters. He says that while he was in camp, so was the winner of a free hunt donated to the membership drive.
Unfortunately, that hunter didn't get his bear, but Dale says that was not the fault of outfitter Frank Smith, who got several hunters black bears that week.

Midmorning Gobblers

A sunrise serenade of gobbling is a wonderful thing for a turkey hunter, but the early-morning scenario isn't your only shot. At times, says Bill Jordan, camouflage czar and hunting fanatic, midmorning hunting may even be better.

"At the peak of breeding season, with many hens out and about, the hunter faces stiff competition," Jordan says. "Usually the hens congregate at or near the gobbler's roost tree in response to his gobbling. When the breeding is done, the hens get back to their daily routine, often leaving the gobbler alone—which he doesn't like very much."

"At such times even hard-hunted gobblers can be vulnerable. Later in the mornings, I tend to cover a lot of ground using crow calls and pileated woodpecker calls to try to start a gobbler up. I also call using yelps, cutting and cackling. Always be in or near cover when you call like a hen. If a nearby gobbler likes what he hears, he may just head straight your way and catch you flat-footed in the open."

Turkey Calls as Locaters

Dick Kirby, veteran turkey hunter and president of Quaker Boy Inc., a leading game call and hunting accessory manufacturer, sometimes gets a gobbler to respond to a gobbler call:

"You can locate a gobbler by challenging him," Kirby reveals. "I have a couple gobbler calls. When I'm not getting results, I shake them to emit either a boss gobble or challenging jake gobble."

Sometimes, using a gobble to locate a tom won't work by itself. "Throw a hen call in there, then gobble on top of that. The gobbler might not be able to hold himself back. His mating instincts take over."

But remember, by using a gobbler call you're posing to be a tom turkey; with any other hunters around, that can put you in a precarious position. "Be extremely careful," Kirby warns. "I suggest you primarily use the gobble early in the morning or early in the evening when you are trying to locate toms on the roost."

Hunter's Survival Quiz

BY J. WAYNE FEARS

*F*ortunately, most hunters will never be in a survival situation, but many will eventually find themselves spending an unplanned night or two in the woods. If it would happen to you, would you have the knowledge to survive?

Here is a test of your survival I.Q. See how you rate. If you get more than 8 correct, you are a survivor; 6 to 8 correct, you need to review a good survival manual; fewer than 6 correct, stay out of the woods until you take a survival course.

1 You are hunting in a wildlife management area on a public hunt and get lost the last afternoon of the hunt. Your best choice for signaling is:

A. Fire 3 shots every 15 minutes.
B. Use your signal mirror.
C. Build a smoky fire.

2 What is the most dangerous climate in which a hunter can become lost or stranded?

A. 20°F, snowing, 5 mph wind
B. 35°F, raining, 15 mph wind
C. 85°F, sunny and dry with 10 mph wind

3 You are deer hunting in an area you have never been in before, so you are using a map and a compass to keep track of your whereabouts. Suddenly you notice that your position doesn't check out with your map. Your compass seems to be inconsistent at pointing to magnetic north. Which is the most likely case?

A. The compass needle is off its pivot.
B. A local iron deposit is pulling the magnetized needle.
C. Your belt buckle is attracting the compass needle.

4 You have been following a heavily used deer trail for about an hour when you realize you don't know where you are. You try to back trail, but you lose the deer trail and know you are really lost. It will be dark within 2 hours. Which of the following would be your best course of action?

A. Find a stream and follow it downhill.
B. Walk uphill and find a high point where you can see the surrounding country.
C. Stop and stay where you are.

158

5 The weather is getting bad, and it's snowing hard. You leave camp in your pickup truck to drive to the top of a nearby mountain to hunt for an hour or so. Four miles from camp, a blizzard sets in, and visibility is poor. Your truck slips off the logging road and gets hopelessly stuck. Which of the following should you do?

A. Stay in your truck and keep warm by running the engine and heater.
B. Get out of your truck and construct a fire and shelter next to the road.
C. Walk back to camp at a pace fast enough to keep you warm.

6 You are duck hunting in a driving rain with a friend. You notice his uncontrollable shivering, and he appears to be in a daze, though still conscious. You suspect hypothermia. You:

A. Give him a strong belt of whiskey to warm him up.
B. Give him warm coffee, tea or water, get him dry clothes and build a fire for warmth.
C. Run him around until he builds up his body temperature.

7 You are on a spring gobbler hunt, and a storm comes up unexpectedly, with lots of lightning. What should you do?

A. Lie in a depressed area in the open away from high trees.
B. Run as fast as you can to your car.
C. Sit under some dense trees so as not to get too wet.

8 Having been lost for two days, you are hungry and have noticed that birds are eating white berries on a low-growing plant near your survival camp. You take the following action.

A. Since birds can safely eat the berries, you assume man can also. You eat them.
B. You eat a few berries and wait a few hours for any adverse effect.
C. You avoid eating the berries since you can't identify the plant.

9 You are in the Yukon and have been lost for four days. There is little to eat, and you are concerned about starvation. How long can you expect to stay alive with no food?

A. 10-15 days
B. 25-30 days
C. 50-60 days

Continued ...

10 Which food gathering method is most effective in a survival situation?

A. Deadfall
B. Snare
C. Fishing line and hooks

11 You and a friend are stranded due to a flood. Your friend has a severe case of diarrhea, and you don't have medicine for him. Which of the following will help his problem?

A. Eating finely ground black charcoal from the campfire.
B. Boiling oak bark and drinking the tea.
C. Eating finely ground leaves from a cedar tree.

12 A solar still is one method of getting drinking water when lost in the desert. What is the maximum amount of water you can expect from a solar still per day?

A. 1 gallon
B. 2 pints
C. $1^1/2$ quarts

13 Which of the following kills the most people each year?

A. Bears
B. Poisonous snakes
C. Stinging insects

Answers:

1. **C.** Gun shots are common in a public hunting area and may not be recognized as a signal. A mirror is good only if an aerial search has been launched. Smoke gets quick attention in a wildlife management area.

2. **B.** Cool temperature, moisture and wind are the combination for hypothermia.

3. C., 4. C.

5. **B.** If you don't run out of gas first, carbon monoxide will likely kill you if you stay in your truck and run the engine and heater.

6. **B.** Exertion and alcohol will only make matters worse. Most hypothermia victims require heat from an external source.

7. A., 8. C., 9. C., 10. C.,

11. A., 12. B., 13. C.

Dealing with Hunter Harassment

BY DAN DIETRICH

All 50 states have laws on the books protecting you from harassment by individuals who want to prevent you from hunting. Fines and prison sentences can be levied against offenders, but you shouldn't take the law into your own hands. Here is what you should do to avoid problems:

- **Practice Avoidance.** Anti-hunters usually announce their protests in advance to hype the public's—and the media's—interest. If you hear of a protest in your area, change plans or enter the area from another access.

- **Keep Your Cool.** Remember that it is senseless to argue with anti-hunters. Instead, redouble your commitment to safety. Make certain that everything the camera sees is exemplary of the safe and ethical hunter. Unload your firearm, leave the action open and keep it pointed in a safe direction. If bowhunting, store all arrows in the quiver. Case all hunting tools as soon as you get back to your vehicle.

- **Notify Authorities.** To increase the possibility of a conviction, walk in several directions to verify that they are following you. Get a good look at each of them. Write down descriptions of each. Write down license plate numbers from their vehicles. Then notify the authorities. Inform them of the harassment, of the law in your state and that you would like to hunt in peace. Write down the officer's name for your records and thank him or her.

- **Take the Anti's on a Trek.** If a group of yelping yahoos insist on shadowing you in the woods, there is nothing wrong with leading them on a little tour. Take them up the highest peak or through the soupiest slough. Make sure you keep giving them a chance to catch up.

- **Communicate the Good News.** Some hunting groups have decided to stage counter media events at the same time the anti's hold their protests. Not only do they present the facts about hunting to the media, but the public see hunters standing up for their rights.

- **Join State or Local Groups.** If you aren't a member of your state hunting or shooting club, join now. These organizations are the ones who face off against anti-hunters in your region. The collective membership can have considerable influence on issues that affect it.

Shiras Moose

ALCES ALCES

OTHER NAMES:
Called elk in Europe, this is the moose of our American West.

CHARACTERISTICS:
Coat dark brown to black; large, overhanging snout; pendant "bell" under throat; antlers massive and flat; tail short; bulls (largest antlered animals in the world) weigh 800 to 1,200 pounds, cows 600 to 800 pounds.

HABITAT:
Variable; in summer, mountain meadows, river valleys, swampy areas, clear cuts; in winter, willow flats or mature coniferous forests; great ability to negotiate deep snow.

FOOD:
Browse, including large saplings; aquatic vegetation.

BEHAVIOR:
Usually solitary but may congregate during rut or on excellent winter range; at home in water, may submerge for 3 to 4 minutes or swim for miles; cows very protective of calves.

REPRODUCTION:
Breed in later September and early October; shed antlers in December or January; one or two russet-brown young without spots. Where moose are scarce, both sexes travel extensively looking for mates. In other areas, both sexes form breeding groups; bulls fight for cows; females usually breed when 2^1/$_2$ years old, but may breed as yearlings on good range.

HUNTING:
Look for Shiras moose in damp areas you might find along a creek, around beaver ponds, in areas of springs and seeps. They're big, but smart! Don't ignore the wind, stalk carefully, be prepared to work to pack out your meat.

SOMETHING TO SHOOT FOR

MOOSE

HUNTER:
Chuck Shellhouse

RESIDENCE:
Monument, CO

WHERE TAKEN:
Alaska

ARMS USED:
Weatherby .340 Mag Rifle

Chuck was hunting units 19 and 17 with guides Glen Trombley and Jeremy Davis out of Lake Country Lodge.

HUNTER:
Charles Whitlock Jr.

RESIDENCE:
Bowling Green, KY

WHERE TAKEN:
Southwest Alaska

ARMS USED:
Weatherby .380 Mag Rifle;
180-Grain Nosler Partition
Bullets

Charles was hunting with guide Joe Hendricks of Fair Chase Hunts.

The Importance of Research

BY BOB ROBB

With limited hunting time, we all need to maximize the time we spend afield where the game is, not where it might be. Research gets you started in the right direction. It's a true part of the hunt—your first steps to your next (or first) elk, deer, bear, antelope, moose, whatever!

STEP ONE: FILES

For instance, into your "elk" file each year put magazine articles, maps, harvest statistics, state game statistics, notes from books and more. Also create separate files for each hunting

The key to any serious on-your-own big game hunter's success, season after season, can be boiled down to two things—planning and hard work. Most hunters get so excited about the actual hunt itself, they forget that without proper planning and meticulous research, their hunt is doomed from the get-go.

state, into which go the current year's hunting regulations and license and tag application procedures.

Keeping everything in organized file folders makes it easier to keep track of the several different hunting trips you might be planning for the coming year as well as hunts you're dreaming about for future years.

STEP TWO: GAME DEPARTMENTS

Contact the game departments of the states you're considering and get the coming year's regulations. Ask the department if they have harvest statistics and tag-drawing odds summaries available.

STEP THREE:
MAPS, MAPS & MORE MAPS

Once you've narrowed your choice of hunting areas down to a general location, it's time for maps. The U.S. Forest Service, Bureau of Land Management, and specific states each have public land maps within specific states that help you locate boundaries, roads, water sources, timbered ridges, trails and trail heads, campgrounds and more.

Later in the process it will be time for U.S. Geological Survey topographic maps. These maps show too small an area for initial planning but are essential for the final planning and hunt execution phases of your trip.

STEP FOUR: PEOPLE

The final stage of the planning process is talking with people. Maps can give you a general overview of the area, but people can fill in the blanks and give you an accurate, up-to-the-minute picture of what the area is really like.

Talk with state game department

biologists whenever possible. I try to work my way down—not up—the departmental flow chart. I don't want the person in charge of half the state—I want the local biologist for a specific forest or drainage I'm considering hunting. The same holds true for game wardens, forest service personnel and so on. Try to talk to people who work right in the hunt area and can fill you in on current conditions and game population numbers.

Also try to talk with local hunters, taxidermists and any other contacts you can think of. I try to ask as many people as I can the same question, then "balance" their answers in my mind.

STEP FIVE: TOPO MAPS

Buy topographic maps of the areas that you're pretty sure you're going to hunt. These help you pinpoint specific creeks, drainages and ridges where research tells you the game should be when you arrive. Topo maps also let you ask the people you're calling very specific questions about the area.

Meticulous research isn't glamorous, it's all part of the chess game, a way to tip the odds for success in your favor and to keep the hunting fire burning during the off-season.

MULE DEER

HUNTER:
Jack Spencer Jr.

RESIDENCE:
Reno, NV

WHERE TAKEN:
Central Idaho

ARMS USED:
Ruger .243 Rifle; 75-Grain
Hollow-Point Bullet

HUNTER:
Ken Keener

RESIDENCE:
Perry, OH

WHERE TAKEN:
Wyoming

ARMS USED:
.270 Weatherby Mag Rifle

Two successful hunters: Ken Keener, right, along with Walter Keener.

TIPS AFIELD

Dress Blue, Be Blue

Hot-weather hunting can be miserable if the mosquitoes are buzzing. According to Tender Corporation, manufacturer of insect repellents, hunters should be color conscious. If you are bird hunting, for instance, and not obliged to wear camouflage, be color conscious. Wear khaki or neutral colors. Mosquitoes are attracted to dark colors, especially blue.

Making a Difference

Most of us would agree: Hunting has made us better people and added dimensions of the outdoors, wildness, adventure, and yes, even some compassion, to life. But what about the kids of today? Will they have the opportunity to be hunters? Only you can make a difference. Here's how:

- If you have your own kids—boys or girls—take the time to take them hunting.

- If your kids are grown and gone, or if you don't have any of your own, find a kid to introduce to hunting.

- Then be smart about hooking them. Start slow. Talk a lot about the hunting. Tell your stories—they will love it and you'll find yourself getting to spin your old yarns again.

- Make sure the new hunter is outfitted properly with a firearm or archery gear they can handle, and clothes, boots and other gear that makes sense.

- Feed them magazines and books with lots of pictures. Answer questions; ask for questions.

As a hunter, you have a gift: knowledge of a grand and storied outdoor sport that needs all the support it can get. And as a hunter, you also have power: the power to change a life (or lives) by introducing young people to the outdoors and hunting.

—Tom Carpenter

RECIPES

Recipes

Rabbit Pie

Apple pie, pumpkin pie, cherry pie, even pecan pie, but what's this with rabbit pie? Try this recipe from the NRA. You'll add it to your list of favorite pies.

Ingredients

1 or 2 rabbits, cut in half
2 bay leaves
2 onions, chopped
2 small carrots, sliced
3 or 4 stalks celery,
    cut into 1-inch pieces
Salt and pepper

1 pie crust, not too rich
4 tbsp. butter or margarine
4 tbsp. flour
2 cups rabbit stock
1 can peas
1 can diced mixed vegetables
2 boiled potatoes, diced

Preparation

Cover rabbit with water and parboil for about 5 minutes. Rinse well and then place in a pot of fresh water. Add bay leaves, onions, carrots, celery, salt and pepper. Cover and cook until meat is fork tender and can be cut from bones—about 1 to 2 hours depending on age of rabbit. Remove meat from bones and cut into bite-sized pieces. Strain stock and reserve. Place pieces of meat in a deep baking dish. For sauce, melt butter in a medium saucepan and blend in flour. Slowly stir in stock. Add to casserole all vegetables and cooked potatoes. After seasoning sauce to taste, pour over meat and vegetables. Cover with pie crust being sure that crust is secured to rim of casserole. Make slits in top of pie crust and bake to a preheated 425°F oven for 20 to 25 minutes or until crust is brown.

NRA Recipe

COYOTE

SOMETHING TO SHOOT FOR

NAME:
Alvie Pay

WHERE TAKEN:
Ohio

ARMS USED:
Hoyt Raptor Bow; Easton
XX78 Arrows with Spitfire
Expandable Broadheads

*Alvie and his son, Seth, squat with the Eastern coyote
Alvie arrowed.*

NAME:
Erich Pfahl

RESIDENCE:
Reading, PA

WHERE TAKEN:
Galeton, Pennsylvania

ARMS USED:
Winchester .30-06 Rifle

Here's Erich with the big coyote he took.

TIPS AFIELD

Solving the Identity Crisis

BY TONY DAWSON

Where black bear and grizzly territories overlap, bear hunters must positively identify the species before taking a shot. When confronted by a bear, every hunter is best off knowing which species he's dealing with.

My experience with both species spans 27 years. Here's how I tell them apart.

CONFUSING COLORS

Black bears are not always black. Shades of brown from chocolate to creamed coffee affect up to 50 percent of some western U.S. and Canada populations. Southeast Alaska harbors two rare color phases, a blue (gray/black) phase "glacier bear" and a white phase "Kermode bear" that's also found in northcoastal British Columbia. Neither inland nor coastal grizzlies are true black, but range in color from dark chocolate to bleached blonde. The trick is to keep from mistaking brown phase black bears for grizzlies—or worse—small grizzlies for brown phase black bears. Occasionally a small darkly colored grizzly might look like a black bear.

One color clue: most black bears have some pure white hair on the chest.

SHAPE & SIZE

More streamlined than grizzlies, black bears have smaller, narrower heads, prominent ears and lack other grizzly traits like "dished" faces and conspicuous shoulder humps. Black bears often look a bit high-rumped compared to a grizzly.

Mature Black Bear

Rump usually higher than front shoulder

Ears are prominent

28"-36"

Short snout

54"-72"

Claws print no more than 1½ inches ahead of toe pads

Larry Anderson Art

On average, black bears are 24 to 30 inches high at the shoulder. Most head-to-tail length is $4^1/_2$ to 6 feet, and they rarely reach 7 feet when standing erect. Roughly human size, mature black bears generally weigh from 125 to 400 pounds.

Coastal and inland grizzlies, once treated as separate species, are now recognized as the same species with size differences due only to diet and habitat. Both are larger than most black bear.

Coastal grizzly bear enjoy longer summers and rich salmon feasts. Some outsized bears will weigh more than half a ton! Though sows are somewhat smaller, size alone easily differentiates these giants from black bears where their ranges overlap.

From Alaska to Wyoming, smaller inland grizzlies endure short, high country summers and a fishless diet of ground squirrels, vegetation and the odd elk or moose calf. Their 200- to 800-pound weights put them closer to black bear size.

The overall size average for coastal and interior grizzlies is 4 feet high at the shoulder and 6 to 7 feet of body length. Standing erect, an average grizzly is 8 feet tall. If color and size confuse you, the broad, massive head and full muzzle of a grizzly is distinctive.

TRACKS

An adult black bear's rear foot is 7 to 9 inches long, and front pads average 5 to 6 inches wide. Claws are short, curved and print less than $1^1/_2$ inches ahead of the toe pads on soft ground. On hard ground, claws may not print at all.

Inland and coastal grizzly tracks show long, straight claws printing $1^1/_2$ to 4 inches ahead of the toe pads. Hind foot prints may be 10 to 14 inches long, and front pads 7 to 10 inches wide.

WHERE YOU FIND THEM

Ask biologists if both bears live where you will hunt. Black bears are

Continued ...

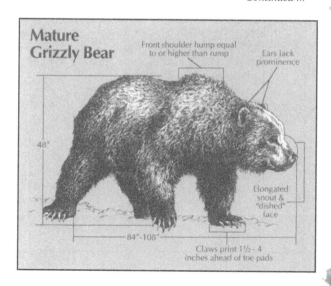

Mature
Grizzly Bear

Front shoulder hump equal to or higher than rump

Ears lack prominence

48"

Elongated snout & "dished" face

84"-108"

Claws print $1^1/_2$ - 4 inches ahead of toe pads

171

found in forested areas in Canada, Alaska and much of the lower 48 states. They are absent from island brown bear strongholds and vast tundra barrens.

Grizzlies live in Alaska, the Yukon and Northwest Territories, British Columbia, Alberta and isolated parts of some Rocky Mountain states.

Black Bear	Grizzly Bear
COLOR	
• Black or shade of brown • Most have some pure white on their chests	• Shade of brown from dark chocolate to bleached blonde
SHAPE, SIZE & APPEARANCE	
• Small, narrow head; prominent ears; high rump • 24 to 30 inches high at shoulder • $4^1/_2$ to 6 feet long • Rarely as tall as 7 feet when standing erect • 125 to 400 pounds	• Large head; elongated snout and "dished" face; conspicuous shoulder humps • 4 feet high at shoulder • 6 to 7 feet long • Average standing height is 8 feet • Inland grizzlies weigh 200 to 800 pounds; coastals can weigh more than half a ton
TRACKS	
• Rear foot is 7 to 9 inches long • Front pads are 5 or 6 inches wide • Short, curved claws print less than $1^1/_2$ inches in front of toe pads on soft ground (may not print at all on hard ground)	• Rear foot is 10 to 14 inches long • Front pads are 7 to 10 inches wide long • Straight claws print $1^1/_2$ to 4 inches in front of the toe pads
RANGE	
• Found in forested areas in Canada, Alaska and much of the Lower 48	• In the U.S, found in Alaska and isolated parts of some Rocky Mountain states; in Canada, found in the Yukon, Northwest Territories, British Columbia and Alberta

SOMETHING TO SHOOT FOR

WHITE-TAILED DEER

HUNTER:
Eddie Norwood

RESIDENCE:
Henderson, NC

WHERE TAKEN:
Vance County,
North Carolina

ARMS USED:
Browning BAR .270 Rifle

HUNTER:
Bill Reynolds

RESIDENCE:
Lafayette, IN

WHERE TAKEN:
Indiana

ARMS USED:
T/C Thunderhawk
.54 Caliber Muzzleloader

Recipes

Pheasant en Creme

Ingredients

4 pheasants
Flour
Salt and Pepper
Butter
Cooking oil
4 cans cream of mushroom
  soup

2 cans light cream
1 cup dry sherry
2 tsp. tarragon leaves
2 tbs. Worcestershire
  sauce
Paprika

Preparation

Cut pheasants in half or section; wash and pat dry. Shake pieces in bag with seasoned flour to coat. Brown lightly in butter and oil. Arrange in shallow baking pan, cut side down. Combine undiluted soup with remaining ingredients, except paprika, in skillet used for browning. Heat and stir until smooth. Pour over pheasant. Sprinkle with paprika. Bake uncovered at 350°F for 1 to 2 hours. Baste several times with sauce during baking. Sprinkle with paprika once more.

Corey Scott
Omaha, NE

Game Bird Care & Prep

There are 3 variations to game-bird care. Some hunters skin, some pluck and others hang.

The decision to field dress should be made as soon as the bird is recovered. If the hunt is short, the temperature not much above 45°F, and the birds will be cleaned soon after the hunt, field dressing can wait. If it will be more than a few hours before the birds will be dressed, remove the entrails and crop. Check local laws before detaching wings, feet or heads in the field.

The issue of hanging or aging birds relates to tenderness. Though it may occasionally help on the rare old cock pheasant, for the most part it is a practice to avoid.

Skinning a bird is definitely quicker and easier than plucking. If you really want to savor the flavor of upland birds, however, take your time and pluck them.

Here's advice from Jerry Waters, who prepares thousands of gamebirds each year:

Cut wings and legs at the joints to avoid jagged edges. Clip wings at the first joint. Make sure kidneys and lungs, as well as shot and feathers, are removed.

Once the birds are clean, soak them in salt water and place in refrigerator for 12 to 24 hours. Adding butter, wine, onions or apples will enhance natural flavors.

If the birds are not destined for the table in the immediate future, they can be frozen, the length of storage time dependent on the freezing and wrapping procedure. A home vacuum sealer can remove all air and prevent freezer burn. You can also freeze birds in water by using plastic containers or waxed milk cartons. Freeze game at 0°F. Do not thaw them in water, nor should you soak them once they've been frozen and thawed. All game birds should be eaten within 9 months of freezing.

SOMETHING TO SHOOT FOR

WILD TURKEY

NAME:
Philip Adams

RESIDENCE:
Plantation, FL

WHERE TAKEN:
Hendry City, Florida

ARMS USED:
Remington 870 12 Gauge Shotgun

*Philip poses with his outstanding
Florida, or Osceola, gobbler.*

NAME:
Dale Petkovsek

RESIDENCE:
Willard, WI

WHERE TAKEN:
Willard, Wisconsin

ARMS USED:
Hunter's Mfg. Magnum Express
Crossbow

*Hunting from a wheelchair, Dale arrowed
this tom with his crossbow!*

How to Approach Downed Game

Approach cautiously and quietly and, if possible, from the back of the animal, suggests the National Bowhunters Education Foundation. Note that this also applies if you hunt with a rifle. Sometimes a wounded animal will suddenly spring to its feet and run.

Try to watch its eyes. Clear or blinking eyes indicate that the animal is still alive. Try to position yourself for another shot.

For gun hunters, a neck shot—or a head shot, if the hunter isn't planning to mount his quarry—is recommended to dispatch the animal. Bowhunters should try to place a shot in the rib cage, then either quietly back off and wait at a distance or wait silently in place, so as not to further spook the animal. It's better to have an extra hole in a skin than to lose a wounded animal.

If the animal's eyes are glazed and unblinking, your quarry is likely dead. Carefully poke the eye area to see if there is any reaction.

SOMETHING TO SHOOT FOR

CATS

NAME:
Stanley Kokolus

RESIDENCE:
Coplay, PA

WHERE TAKEN:
Salmon, Idaho

ARMS USED:
Muzzleloader

Stanley took this cougar while guided by Shane McAfee of Castle Creek Outfitters.

NAME:
John Speelman

RESIDENCE:
Bryan, Texas

WHERE TAKEN:
Parker County, Texas

ARMS USED:
.243 Rifle

John was hunting on the Powell Ranch in Weathorford, TX, when he connected on this bobcat.

178

NAME:
Bernard R. Harvey

RESIDENCE:
Grundy, VA

WHERE TAKEN:
Santa Rosa Mountains, Nevada

ARMS USED:
Ruger Mini 14 .223 caliber Rifle;
Winchester 55-Grain Bullets

Hunting with Gary Coleman, a guide for Blackrock Outfitters, Bernard got this handsome mountain lion.

NAME:
Jim Olson

RESIDENCE:
Isanti, MN

WHERE TAKEN:
Nakusp, British Columbia

ARMS USED:
Ruger .44 Mag Rifle; 240-
Grain Hand Loads

Jim got this big mountain lion while hunting with Ken Robins of Whatshan Guides.

Use Your Scope as a Rangefinder

BY LARRY WEISHUHN

i.e.
8X@
400 Yards — 40 Inches —

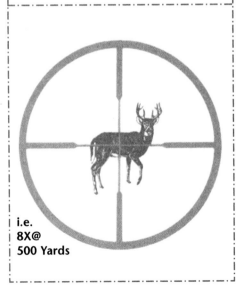

i.e.
8X@
500 Yards

Variable power scopes with duplex crosshairs can be used as accurate, in-the-field rangefinders.

First, determine the distance covered by the thin, inside "cross" of the crosshairs at a set power and set distance. Let's say at 8X that distance is 40 inches at 400 yards.

Next, determine the body length of the game animal. Let's say an average whitetail has a body length of 40 inches. Thus, if an average whitetail standing broadside fits between the thicker portions of the crosshairs, the deer is 400 yards distant.

This technique is especially helpful at longer distances where you question whether the animal is within your effective range. If, at 8X, the whitetail is smaller than the thin, inside crosshairs, he is more than 400 yards away.

Caution: Don't assume that every scope is the same. The distance covered by the thin, inside crosshairs can vary depending on the manufacturer, the scope model, the power setting, and so on.

TIPS AFIELD

10 Turkey Hunting Tips for Safety & Success on Public Land

BY JOHN PHILLIPS

1 Assume that every sound you hear is made by another hunter. Wait until you actually see the bird before snapping the safety off.

2 Wear a hunter-orange hat and vest to cover your camo clothing whenever you are on the move.

3 Never wear clothing or gear that is red, white or blue. That includes items like handkerchiefs and underwear.

4 After bagging a tom, try to cover it completely for transport out of the woods, preferably in a hunter-orange bag or wrap.

5 Learn which areas and times are heavily pressured. Avoid them.

6 Never use a gobble call.

7 Take a position that affords good visibility in all directions.

8 Sit with your back to a tree large enough that hunters approaching from the rear won't see small movements around the side of the tree.

9 Never try to "stalk" a turkey.

10 Check, check and recheck your target and what lies beyond before pulling the trigger.

Pattern Your Shotgun

Tiger Woods wouldn't tee up at the Masters with a set of clubs he'd never swung before. He may be the best at what he does, but he doesn't rely on talent to overcome ignorance of his "tools'" capabilities.

In the same way, it doesn't make sense to take a shotgun afield if you don't know exactly where it shoots. Seldom does a shotgun center its pattern exactly on target. Most times the density of the pattern will be high, low or slightly off to the side of the point of aim. It's essential to know where your shotgun centers its pattern so that you can either compensate or have the gun adjusted.

"The industry standard for patterning is a 30-inch circle at 40 yards," describes shooting expert Joe Ventimiglia. "But you should set up for the distance you'll be shooting most often. For instance, 40 yards is too long if you're patterning an open choke and No. 6 for pheasants or No. 8 for grouse."

Your first shot should be at a well-marked center on a clean sheet of wallboard or plywood to get a general idea of where your pattern is going. Then use paper—two sheets of butcher paper taped lengthwise is wide enough. Mark the center and shoot.

If you're patterning for wingshooting, don't take careful aim. Instead, snap the gun to your shoulder, get the sight picture and slap the trigger, just as if you were in the field. If you're patterning a turkey load or buckshot, take careful aim, as you would do in an actual hunting situation. Take at least five shots at five different pieces of paper before making any adjustments.

Recipes

Smoked Venison & Apple Sausage

Ingredients

3 lbs. venison, diced
1 1/2 lbs. fatback, diced
1 cup apple, small diced
1 1/2 tsp. ground white pepper
1/2 tsp. ginger
1/2 tsp. nutmeg

1 tsp. curing salt
1/2 tsp. sage
1/2 oz. salt
1/2 pint cold water
Medium hog casings,
   as needed

Preparation

Sprinkle spices over meat. Blend well. Grind meat using a fine die. Mix ground meat and apple in a mixer for 1 minute. Add cold water while mixing. Stuff meat into the hog casing. Smoke sausage until the internal temperature reaches 155°F. Remove sausage from smoker and shower with cold water until internal temperature is 110°F. Refrigerate for use.

Dwayne Spencer
Middletown, PA

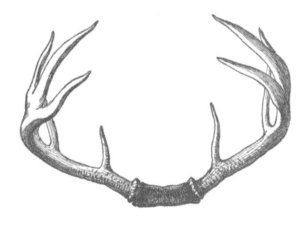

What Is a Wildcat?

A wildcat is not necessarily what you think if you are thinking it is a bobcat. Have you ever heard of a wildcat cartridge? Do you know what it is?

Winchester, Remington and their predecessors have designed and developed the majority of the commercial rifle and pistol calibers available today—but not all of them.

The remainder of the calibers on the market often started life as wildcats, that is, factory cartridges reformed or fireformed by enterprising amateur ballisticians into a different version of itself. The wildcat cartridge is not, by definition, produced commercially. The primary reason for its invention and continued existence was to obtain higher velocity and more striking energy than a conventional cartridge.

Many very popular commercial cartridges actually started life as wildcat loadings. The .35 Whelen, for example, is a .30-06 case resized to accept a .357 bullet, and the .22-250 is a Savage .250-3000 necked down to .224 caliber. One of the more popular small-bore centerfire cartridges today, the .243 Winchester, started out as a 6mm bullet that gun writer Warren Page, long-time shooting editor of *Field & Stream*, modified into something called the .240 Page Super Pooper.

Match the Bullet to the Cartridge

A quality bullet can make the difference when conditions are extreme. Here, bullets were fired at reduced velocity to simulate long-range hits.

Even though different cartridges may take the same bullets, not all the cartridges will extract the same bullet performance.

Generally speaking and with all else being equal, the larger the capacity of the case, the heavier the bullet you should use. For example, when hunting deer, a 140-grain bullet is a good choice for the 7mm-08 Rem., but a 160-grain may be far better for the 7mm Rem.

Smaller cases simply don't have the powder capacity to utilize heavy bullets well. For example, the 200-grain is an excellent weight for the .300 magnums, but trying to use it in a .308 will result in disappointment.

It is always best to match the cartridge to both the game being hunted and the expected shooting distances, and then match the bullet to all three. This, of course, applies to bullet design as well as weight.

—Bryce Towsley

WATERFOWL

SOMETHING TO SHOOT FOR

NAME:
William Niemann

RESIDENCE:
Minot, ND

WHERE TAKEN:
North Dakota

ARMS USED:
12 Gauge Shotgun

William and two big Canada geese.

NAME:
Greg Eames

RESIDENCE:
Menan, ID

WHERE TAKEN:
Tetonia, Idaho

ARMS USED:
Remington 870
12 Gauge Shotgun

Greg proudly displays his giant sandhill crane.

TIPS AFIELD

The Gobbler Will Tell You How to Call

"Listen to the gobbler," says camouflage manufacturer and well-traveled turkey hunter Bill Jordon. "A gobbler will often 'tell' you how he wants to be called. In general, your calling should match his mood. A hot, excited gobbler is best matched with an imitation of a hot, excited hen, at least at first. A less fired-up bird is generally a candidate for more conservative calling. But you might try an occasional aggressive call to see if you can fire him up."

"When the gobbler comes right back to your call or, even better, 'cuts you off' by gobbling while you are calling, you've got his attention, and you may well get him. Usually when a gobbler starts heading your way, he quits gobbling or gobbles less frequently."

"If you call at this time you are making him *stop coming* to respond, and he may 'hang up' waiting for the 'hen' to come to him. When he gets in close, it's your turn to play hard to get. Call softly and infrequently to keep him interested and looking for you."

Did You know?

Federal excise taxes on sporting firearms and ammunition, first proposed by the industry in 1937, and federal excise taxes on hand guns, supported by the industry, raise more than $155 million annually for wildlife management programs.

More than $3 billion has been raised for conservation since these taxes were enacted.

Start Shooting Early

You need to start shooting and sighting in your rifles in midsummer for best results in the fall. That's advice Larry Weishuhn, expert whitetail hunter and Team Realtree member, gives over and over again.

"First off, if any mechanical problems crop up, you still have time to get them fixed. If you've mounted a new scope, had your rifle bedded, changed ammo or made any other significant change in your shooting rig, starting your shooting sessions early gets the kinks worked out," Weishuhn says.

"Gun writers are particularly sensitive to this because we change our gear so often when testing new optics, new loads and new guns. All sorts of things crop up: mounts that are incompatible with scope or gun, ammo that doesn't shoot as expected and new guns with mechanical difficulties that range from major to minor."

"A problem discovered two or three months before the season allows time for correction. However, two or three days before opening day, it's a different story," Weishuhn concludes.

Larry L. Weishuhn

Choosing a Taxidermist

BY BARBARA ELLIOTT

*H*ere are 10 questions to ask a taxidermist when deciding upon the one to preserve your special game bird or animal:

1   Do you specialize in any particular species of game animal?

2   How many mounts do you do each year of the species I'll be hunting?

3   How long will it take for you to finish my trophy mount?

4   Do you do your own tanning or do you send the hides elsewhere to be tanned?

5   What method of skinning should I use to give you the best cape and hide to work with?

6   Do you recommend salting capes and hides or is it better to freeze them if possible?

7   Do you prefer the hide folded or rolled until I can get it to you?

8   Does your price include crating, shipping and delivery of the finished mount?

9   Do you treat your mounts against insect damage?

10   What special things should I do to care for my mount at home?

Recipes

Mild Mexico BBQ

Ingredients

6 lbs. ground venison
3 tbsp. margarine
1½ cups onion, chopped
¾ cup celery, chopped
⅓ cup plus tbsp. lemon juice
2 tbsp. plus 1 tsp. wine vinegar

2 (15 oz.) cans tomato puree
⅓ cup packed sugar
1 (16 oz.) can tomato paste
½ tsp. red cayenne pepper
1 (16 oz.) can water
½ tsp. cumin seed

Preparation

Brown onion in margarine and add venison. Brown venison, drain and add remaining ingredients, crushing cumin seeds first. Simmer for 45 minutes. Fills 40 large hamburger buns. Prep Time: 1 hour.
Serves: 20-40.

Michael Wagner
Rockport, IL

GAME BIRDS & SMALL GAME

NAME:
Alex Lombard

RESIDENCE:
Queensbury, NY

WHERE TAKEN:
Queensbury, New York

ARMS USED:
20 Gauge Shotgun

Alex didn't have to go far from home to find a forest that would yield to him this fine brace of gray squirrels.

NAME:
Shaun Decker

RESIDENCE:
Norwalk, CA

WHERE TAKEN:
Perris, California

ARMS USED:
Remington 11-84 .410
Shotgun

Shaun gave the pheasants at the Four Winds Pheasant Club a particularly sporting chance by downing these birds with a .410.

Wood Duck

Aix sponsa

OTHER NAMES:

Woodie, squealer, acorn duck

CHARACTERISTICS:

Males (drakes) are our most colorful and beautiful duck, in most hunters' opinions. The elegant plumage combination of rich purple-red chest, blue-white-green-and-purple crested head and gray-streaked flanks are unmatched. A hen is gray but still pretty; look for the white ring around her eye.

HABITAT:

Wood ducks love water and woodlands, and where the two come together is where you'll find the ducks. If oak trees are around, so much the better. You will find woodies out in the more open marshes and other waterways as well, but they are certainly our most forest oriented duck.

FOOD:

Acorns are the preferred food, but nuts and seeds from other trees and shrubs are also eaten.

BEHAVIOR:

Wood ducks don't quack like other ducks. Rather, they make a whistling "sque-eek sque-eek" squeal. You'll hear this when a woodie flushes.

NESTING:

True to their forest mentality, wood duck hens nest in tree holes. Once the eggs hatch and the ducklings are ready, they jump out one-by-one to land and bounce once or twice on the ground, get up, and follow their mother to water. Man-made nest boxes are important to wood duck survival.

HUNTING STRAGETIES:

Jump shooting wood ducks is fun. Walk a streambank, sneaking up to bends and cutbanks with your shotgun at the ready. Set up a blind in some flooded timber or on the banks of a wooded stream or one of its backwaters; set out some little wood duck decoys and use a wood duck whistle call.

—Tom Carpenter